JEFFREY MIRON

U.S. FISCAL IMBALANCE

CATO INSTITUTE

WASHINGTON, D.C.

For information about reprint permission, please contact
Cato Institute
1000 Massachusetts Ave., N.W.
Washington, D.C. 20001

Published by Cato Institute Press.

eISBN 978-1-939709-98-1 (digital)
ISBN 978-1-944424-11-4 (print)

Cover design by Jon Meyers.
www.cato.org

Contents

Introduction

John Allison[*]

Early in my banking career I was a financial analyst. My role was to study financial statements and evaluate whether or not a business was sound. My firm also provided financing for municipal governments. In this work, we relied on the Generally Accepted Accounting Principles (GAAP) for businesses. The GAAP system had many flaws, but the accounting system for governmental entities was even more misleading—and unlike GAAP, the government's accounting system has not been improved.

A major misleading factor was that neither government nor businesses had to account for all of their future commitments. This system was particularly misleading for heavily unionized industries that had extremely generous retirement plans and postretirement health care subsidies. It was even more misleading for government entities that offered their employees extraordinary postretirement benefits.

Leaders of unionized companies often bought short-term peace with the unions by making commitments that future managers would have to pay for, especially because the GAAP system did not reflect this future cost. Of course, the temptation for politicians was—and still is—even greater. They are almost uniformly driven by short-term concerns, with a focus on the next election. Little incentive is needed for politicians to sacrifice the future for the present.

The problems in municipal accounting are magnified dramatically at the level of the federal government because of Social Security, Medicare, Medicaid, and other entitlement programs. The numbers are much, much larger, and the potential negative consequences much, much more severe.

[*]John Allison is the retired president and CEO of the Cato Institute and retired chairman and CEO of BB&T Corporation.

1

GAAP accounting standards about future commitments for businesses' postretirement benefits have changed significantly, but the federal government's accounting system, or lack thereof, remains the same. Businesses must compare the estimated value of assets in their retirement plans with the liabilities owed by the plans and must use a present value approach. Issues remain about assumed earnings rates and discount rates, but this approach is a major improvement. A number of companies, especially unionized firms, substantially underfund their postretirement commitments, which could create serious problems for those businesses. Moreover, a government-required pension plan insurance program (the Pension Benefit Guaranty Corporation) could be jeopardized if current accounting practices and this "fiscal myopia" continue.

Few people realize that General Motors (GM) was effectively bankrupt before the recent financial crisis. Knowing that the firm was on the verge of failing helps explain some of the management decisions made at GM before the crisis. The changes to GAAP forced GM to demonstrate the unfunded liabilities of its extremely generous employee postretirement benefit plans. The deficiencies in the funding for the plans were huge. When those liabilities were properly accounted for, GM was shown to have a massive negative net worth. One reason that GM could not obtain private financing during the financial crisis was that it was practically bankrupt before the crisis. It survived thanks only to extremely loose precrisis lending practices.

Despite political rationalizations to the contrary, GM did go bankrupt during the financial crisis. The unique aspect of this bankruptcy was that the long-established order of claims in bankruptcy was realigned under pressure from government officials. Unionized autoworkers' retirement plans benefited at the expense of other bondholders, including public employee pension plans.

Unfortunately, a lesson in the GM example may apply to a number of governmental entities. If the GAAP accounting practices currently applied to businesses were applied to those entities, some of them would have the equivalent of a tremendous negative net worth. (This accounting change is theoretically in process but does not apply to the federal government, which is not a surprise). Will this negative net worth affect the entities' ability to obtain financing when it becomes evident? If a government entity gets in financial trouble, will its creditors be treated according to long-established priorities—or will politics determine how much each creditor receives?

Most people believe accounting standards are set by an independent organization. In fact, accounting standards are practically controlled by the Securities and Exchange Commission, a federal government agency. To believe that accounting standards are not influenced by politics is, frankly, naive. Unfortunately, the last place to expect transparent or unbiased accounting is at the federal level.

Business-type GAAP for government entities would be a major improvement, but proper government accounting requires an even more sophisticated approach. In the United States, government agencies, especially at the federal level, have unique characteristics and very long-term commitments. The fundamental question for the government is, therefore, balancing the most likely present value of future revenues against the most likely present value of future expenses. The range of probable outcomes should also be considered. If the present value of future revenues exceeds the present value of future expenses, then the government is probably in sound fiscal condition.

If the present value of future expenses exceeds the present value of future revenues, the government could have a problem. Economists generally define a deficiency of this nature as a "fiscal imbalance." (This is an economic concept as opposed to an accounting concept, but proper accounting should of course be driven by economics.) If the fiscal imbalance is large, the government definitely faces a problem that requires an eventual solution. Either future revenues will have to increase or future expenses will need to decrease—or a combination of both.

Jeffrey Miron, the director of economic studies at the Cato Institute and the director of undergraduate studies in the Department of Economics at Harvard University, has performed a comprehensive analysis of America's fiscal imbalance. Alarmingly, he finds that the fiscal imbalance of the federal government now stands at a staggering $117.9 trillion. Put another way, the present value of future U.S. expenses exceeds the present value of future revenues by $117.9 trillion. That is a very, very, very large deficit. It is 6.8 times the nation's annual gross domestic product and vastly more than the reported U.S. government (net) debt of $13.1 trillion. It materially exceeds the total estimated value of all private wealth in the United States, which is approximately $63.5 trillion.

Dr. Miron has also performed a sensitivity analysis to see how the fiscal imbalance varies under different economic assumptions. Regrettably, unless fundamental changes to public policy and entitlement spending are enacted, the fiscal imbalance will remain huge. Some liberal economists claim the fiscal imbalance can be cured by raising taxes on wealthy individuals. That strategy absolutely would not work and could even be counterproductive by slowing growth. Some conservative economists believe the fiscal imbalance can be fixed by accelerating growth. Although faster economic growth would be advantageous, it would do little to resolve America's deep fiscal imbalance.

Although a more rational tax strategy and faster economic growth can chip away at our country's fiscal imbalance, the only way to fundamentally alleviate it is to significantly reduce future commitments for government spending. The primary causes of the massive fiscal imbalance are entitlement programs combined with the aging of the U.S. population. Those two factors help explain why our current fiscal imbalance is so dramatically different from past fiscal challenges that our government has faced. Various entitlement programs are reaching their maturity as baby boomers retire. The financial challenges accelerate as the bulk of the baby boomers approach age 80 and require greater health care.

Specifically, America's fiscal imbalance is mainly driven by government health care entitlement programs: Medicare, Medicaid, the Affordable Care Act, and related health care costs. The cost of those programs must be materially reduced. Otherwise, the fiscal imbalance cannot be managed, thus leading to major fiscal challenges in the future. The good news is that a number of solutions to the health care cost problem could both reduce costs and improve health care quality at the same time. Health Savings Accounts and market-driven insurance policies (including high-deductible options) are just two examples. However, the goal of this report is not to offer a comprehensive set of solutions but rather to prove that the U.S. government faces a major problem that must be fixed. The longer politicians wait, the more difficult the solution will be. Evading the threat of fiscal meltdown will not make it go away.

Dr. Miron's analysis clearly outlines the magnitude of the fiscal imbalance, the financial risk we carry as a nation, and the limits of proposed solutions. The easy solutions will not work. What is necessary instead is a fundamental change in government entitlement policies, especially in health care. The first step is recognizing we have a problem and understanding the nature of that challenge. The next step is creating a consensus among academic, business, and political opinion leaders around the need for reform. We all share a fundamental moral obligation to future generations to deal with this challenge in a timely way—the sooner, the better.

Fiscal Imbalance: A Primer

Jeffrey Miron

Department of Economics, Harvard University, and the Cato Institute

Executive Summary

The concept of fiscal imbalance is familiar to economists but less so to policymakers, politicians, and the public. Yet understanding this concept is essential to rational discussion of government financial health.

This paper provides a primer on government fiscal imbalance. The material is not new, and the presentation does not aim at those familiar with the topic. Instead, the paper reviews key principles and fundamental implications; it targets those who are interested in understanding the true state of government financial health but puzzled by apparently conflicting claims about whether the major economies are going bankrupt. This primer does not resolve those conflicts, but by explicating the concept of fiscal imbalance, and reviewing the relevant facts, the discussion provides a framework for evaluating the competing claims.

Introduction

Are governments spending beyond their means? If so, by how much? Are the United States and Europe on paths to becoming Greece? Why? Because of excessive health and retirement spending, or slow growth, or fiscal stimulus, or something else? Did imbalances arise recently, or have they just been ignored? Does waiting to make adjustments help or hurt? And has the slowdown in health cost inflation made current fiscal worries less pressing?

All these questions concern fiscal imbalance, which is the difference between a government's planned spending and projected revenues. The concept of fiscal imbalance is familiar to economists but less so to policymakers, politicians, and the public. Yet understanding this concept is essential to rational discussion of government financial health.

This paper provides a primer on government fiscal imbalance. The material is not new, and the presentation does not aim at those familiar with the topic. Instead, the paper reviews key principles and fundamental implications; it targets those who are interested in the questions posed above but puzzled by conflicting claims on these issues. This primer does not resolve those conflicts, but by explicating the concept of fiscal imbalance, and reviewing the relevant facts, the discussion provides a framework for evaluating competing claims.

The remainder of the paper proceeds as follows. The first section defines "fiscal imbalance" and relates this concept to other concerns about government expenditure. The next section reviews why neither the debt nor the deficit is an accurate measure of fiscal imbalance. Subsequent sections first explain how to compute fiscal imbalance and then review estimates of fiscal imbalance for the United States and Europe. The final two sections discuss policy options going forward and address the questions about imbalance posed above. An appendix discusses calculation of fiscal imbalance in the presence of uncertainty about future expenditures and revenues.

What Is Fiscal Imbalance?

Economies face three main issues in choosing the amount and kind of government expenditure. One is whether expenditure on a given program generates benefits that exceed costs. A second is whether policymakers should raise expenditure during recessions on the basis of Keynesian stabilization concerns.

Fiscal imbalance is about a third issue: whether a government can continue forever to make the expenditure implied by its existing policies, given the predicted revenues under those policies and the government's explicit debt. Governments, like individuals and businesses, can borrow and therefore spend more than their revenues in any given period. But, like individuals and businesses, governments cannot do so indefinitely. If lenders believe a government will not raise sufficient revenue to repay its borrowing, those lenders will, at some point, stop rolling over that government's debt or do so only at higher and higher interest rates (which makes the problem worse). Thus, governments face the constraint that the "sum" of expenditure over the infinite future cannot exceed the ability to raise revenue over that same future. Fiscal imbalance aims to measure the divergence between the planned long-run expenditure path and the projected long-run revenue path; estimated imbalance shows how much additional tax revenue a government must raise, over the long haul, to afford its planned expenditures.

Fiscal Imbalance vs. Evaluation of Specific Policies

Fiscal imbalance answers a different question than whether expenditure for a particular program is desirable. Such analyses, the domain of standard microeconomics, should address all the consequences (fiscal and otherwise) of making the expenditure. One negative of any policy or program is the opportunity cost of the required expenditure; a second is the distortions caused by the taxation necessary to fund the expenditure. These negatives, along with any unintended consequences, must be balanced against any benefits achieved by the program.

But the microeconomic analysis of a specific program does not, and should not, assume that the revenue needed to pay for the expenditure must come from the same program. Most government policies that involve expenditure do not contain their own funding (e.g., Medicaid, Temporary Assistance for Needy Families [welfare], the Supplemental Nutrition Assistance Program [food stamps], the National Science Foundation, the Federal Trade Commission, or the National Endowment for the Arts).[1] Moreover, whether a program is desirable bears no

---

[1] Some programs do have a dedicated funding source; for example, the Interstate Highway System gets (most of) its funding from the federal gasoline tax. As with other programs, however, the link between the source of funds and the use of funds is purely

relation to whether that program is "balanced" on its own. National defense and criminal justice require substantial expenditure while providing little direct revenue, so these programs are fiscally imbalanced. But most people endorse such programs, at least to some degree. As long as a government can raise revenue from whatever sources to afford its overall expenditure, the government can be in balance even though individual programs are not.

Thus, fiscal imbalance is about the sustainability of a government's overall expenditure plans; the fiscal imbalance of any individual program is not well defined. Many analyses nevertheless compute the balance of specific programs, such as Social Security or Medicare. As currently operated, these programs make expenditures and raise revenue via dedicated payroll and other taxes, and these programs operate trust funds that accumulate these revenues and pay out the expenditures. The difference between the planned expenditure and the expected revenues, minus any balance in the trust fund, indicates how much additional tax revenue must be collected to make these programs "solvent."

But solvency is not meaningful in these cases because their trust funds could borrow from the rest of the government if the balances in the funds were negative. Equivalently, Congress could decide to pay Social Security or Medicare benefits out of income tax or other revenues. Indeed, Medicare is already funded partially out of general revenues.[2]

Stated differently, any dollar of revenue, regardless of its source, can pay for any kind of expenditure. Congress could have created a Social Security or Medicare program with benefits paid out of general revenues. Assuming the total revenue from all sources (Social Security, Medicare, personal income, corporate income, inheritance, and excise taxes, plus asset forfeitures, license fees, leases, and so on) were the

---

an accounting artifact; nothing prevents Congress from allocating general revenues to highway construction, as it did in 2008, 2009, and 2010. See Eric M. Weiss, "Highway Trust Fund Is Nearly Out of Gas," *Washington Post*, September 6, 2008; and "President Signs Bill Providing 9-Month Extension, $19.5 Billion for Highway Trust Fund," *Washington Post*, March 19, 2010.

[2] See the Medicare website at http://www.medicare.gov/about-us/how-medicare-is-funded/medicare-funding.html. In 2014, general revenues accounted for 41.28 percent of Medicare funding. See *2014 Annual Report of the Boards of Trustees of the Federal Hospital Insurance and Federal Supplementary Medical Insurance Trust Funds*, Table II.B1 (Washington, D.C., July 28, 2014), http://www.cms.gov/Research-Statistics-Data-and-Systems/Statistics-Trends-and-Reports/ReportsTrustFunds/downloads/tr2014.pdf.

same, the fiscal balance of the United States federal government would be the same, even though Social Security and Medicare would have huge imbalances.[3, 4]

Fiscal Imbalance and Fiscal Stimulus

Fiscal imbalance also addresses a different question than whether increased expenditure during recessions—fiscal stimulus—is a desirable or effective way to moderate the business cycle fluctuations of the aggregate economy.[5] The standard Keynesian argument for such expenditure accepts that stimulus will normally worsen fiscal imbalance but asserts the additional imbalance is a necessary evil.

Regardless of whether fiscal stimulus is good policy, however, such expenditure increases are temporary, so their impact on fiscal imbalance, which includes expenditures and revenues over the infinite fu-

---

[3] The fact that revenues are fungible across programs is also why the creation of personal accounts in which Social Security participants can save some or all of their Social Security payroll taxes does nothing to "save Social Security" or improve overall fiscal balance. Holding the path of promised Social Security benefits constant, a reduction in Social Security taxes caused by putting some of these revenues in private accounts just means that Congress will have to raise other taxes to honor its benefit promises. Thus, Social Security participants end up paying the same amount in taxes overall, so their savings do not change. This makes it irrelevant whether the return on private investment opportunities is greater than the so-called return from Social Security taxes; participants have no extra savings with which to earn higher returns. See Kevin M. Murphy and Finis Welch, "Perspectives on the Social Security Crisis and Proposed Solutions," *American Economic Review* (1998):142–50; John Geanakoplos, Olivia S. Mitchell, and Stephen P. Zeldes, "Social Security Money's Worth," National Bureau of Economic Research [NBER] Working Paper no. 6722, 1998; John Geanakoplos, Olivia S. Mitchell, and Stephen P. Zeldes, "Would a Privatized Social Security System Really Pay a Higher Rate of Return?" *Framing the Social Security Debate: Values, Politics, and Economics* (Washington, D.C.: Brookings Institution Press, 1998), p. 137.

[4] A related point is that state and local employee pension plans typically place contributions from employers and employees into a fund from which future benefits are later paid. Thus one can calculate the amount of expenditure required to honor the pension plan's commitments and compare that to the amount of accumulated assets. Any gap indicates an imbalance in the pension plan, considered in isolation. But since state or local governments can, in principle, use any revenues to pay pension benefits, these governments can be in balance overall so long as their planned revenue from all sources is sufficient to pay both the pension and nonpension expenditure implied by their current policies.

[5] The evidence on whether spending stimuli dampen recessions is mixed; for a review, see Valerie A. Ramey, "Can Government Purchases Stimulate the Economy?" *Journal of Economic Literature* 49, no. 3 (2011): 673–85.

ture, is modest.[6] The American Recovery and Reinvestment Act of 2009, for example, was a one-time expenditure of roughly $800 billion. As discussed below, fiscal imbalance in the United States is measured in the tens of trillions. Thus, even as large a stimulus as the ARRA has only a minor impact on fiscal imbalance.[7]

Fiscal Imbalance Is about Sustainability

Fiscal imbalance thus differs from both standard microeconomic analysis of particular programs and from standard macroeconomic analysis of stimulus spending. Fiscal imbalance instead measures the sustainability of a government's current policies, given the future expenditures implied by those policies and the projected revenues from all sources. A government in fiscal balance can continue its current policies indefinitely; a government in imbalance will have to change its policies, at least eventually.

Stated differently, fiscal balance is a necessary condition for the total amount of government expenditure to make sense; fiscal balance is not, however, a sufficient condition for any individual program or policy, or for the overall level of expenditure, to be desirable government policy. That is, being in balance does not mean the expenditure for current policies is worthwhile, merely that the expenditure is not unaffordable. Just as an individual with sufficient income can make unwise expenditures without going bankrupt, or a healthy business can waste money on executive perks without substantially reducing its market valuation, so too a healthy economy can afford policies that might not be desirable, so long as the government is not too extravagant overall.

Any calculation of fiscal balance must define what is meant by "continuation of current policy," and the right approach is not clear-cut. Continuation of current policy on national defense, for example, might

---

[6] Under some conditions, a fiscal stimulus might raise future output and, therefore, tax revenue enough to offset the stimulus, thereby improving fiscal balance on net. See J. Bradford DeLong and Lawrence H. Summers, "Fiscal Policy in a Depressed Economy," *Brookings Papers on Economic Activity* (Spring 2012): 233–97. For critiques, see within that article Martin Feldstein and Valerie A. Ramey, "Comments and Discussion," *Brookings Papers on Economic Activity* (Spring 2012): 275–90.

[7] The Keynesian argument for additional expenditure is also distinct from desirability of a particular program on microeconomic grounds. According to the textbook Keynesian model, additional expenditure can increase output, and by more than the increase in expenditure (via the multiplier), even if this expenditure is on inherently worthless goods or services (paying people to dig ditches and fill them up).

11

mean holding nominal expenditure constant, or real expenditure constant, or real expenditure per capita constant, or spending relative to gross domestic product (GDP) constant, or the past trend in any of these constant. Which approach one adopts matters a great deal.

This issue is especially relevant for entitlement programs like Social Security or Medicare. These policies "promise" benefits to citizens who meet specific criteria, and unless Congress changes the law, these policies continue forever. So the (implicit) promises are not just to existing generations but to all future generations as well. This is a natural interpretation of "continuing current policy" in the context of entitlement programs.

Some analyses of Social Security nevertheless calculate a different but related measure of imbalance.[8] This alternative calculation is typically the difference between the accrued benefits and the balance in the trust fund. This amount, often referred to as the maximum transition cost, is the amount of additional tax revenue that would be necessary to eliminate Social Security without reneging on existing promises.[9]

Measures of the difference between the expenditure and revenue of specific programs are different from fiscal imbalance, which as defined

---

[8] See, for example, John Geanakoplos and Stephen P. Zeldes, "Market Valuation of Accrued Social Security Benefits," in *Measuring and Managing Federal Financial Risk*, ed. Deborah Lucas (Chicago: University of Chicago Press, 2011), pp. 213–33; or Alexander W. Blocker, Laurence J. Kotlikoff, and Stephen A. Ross, "The True Cost of Social Security," NBER Working Paper no. 14427, 2008.

[9] Similarly, calculations of the imbalances in state and local pension plans often address the cost of honoring promises to those who have already made contributions to the pension system rather than examining the cost of continuing the pension plan forever. See, for example, Robert Novy-Marx and Joshua D. Rauh, "Public Pension Promises: How Big Are They and What Are They Worth?" *Journal of Finance* 66, no. 4 (2011): 1207–45. These calculations are relevant to state and local governments that wish to reduce pension expenditure to help balance their budgets. Under the laws of most states, these governments are legally obligated to pay promised benefits to former employees already receiving benefits and, to a lesser degree, to current employees who are partially or fully vested. See Jeffrey R. Brown and David W. Wilcox, "Discounting State and Local Pension Liabilities," *American Economic Review* 99, no. 2 (2009): 538–42. Nothing dictates, however, that these governments offer the same or any pension plan to future employees; these prospective employees could instead be offered a 401k plan or higher salary in lieu of pensions (or offered lower total compensation, if sufficient qualified applicants are available). Thus, for some questions, it is natural to compute the imbalance implied by this more limited set of promises. See, for example, Robert Novy-Marx and Joshua D. Rauh, "Policy Options for State Pension Systems and Their Impact on Plan Liabilities," *Journal of Pension Economics and Finance* 10, no. 2 (2011): 173–94.

here includes the entire government and continuation of current policies into the infinite future. The amount of expenditure on a specific program contributes to any fiscal imbalance calculation, as does any revenue generated. But such program-specific imbalances only indicate that, to continue the path of planned expenditure for that program, revenues from other sources will be necessary; these program-specific imbalances do not, by themselves, mean that overall government is fiscally unsound.

The Deficit and the Debt Are Inadequate Measures of Fiscal Imbalance

The traditional measures of government fiscal health are the current deficit and the outstanding debt. The deficit equals current expenditure, including interest payments on the debt, minus current revenue.[10] The debt equals the sum of all past deficits and surpluses. Larger deficits and a larger debt imply a less fiscally balanced government, other things equal; but a long literature explains why these concepts are incomplete measures of a government's fiscal situation. I review these points here.[11]

The deficit has two limitations as a measure of a government's financial situation. A deficit can arise from infinite combinations of expenditures and revenues, so long as expenditure and revenue differ by the same amount. High taxes and high expenditure likely have different implications for government financial health than low taxes and low expenditure, since the levels of expenditure and revenue both affect economic growth.[12]

---

[10] Government revenue consists mainly of taxes but also fees, fines, forfeitures, legal settlements, and more.

[11] See Laurence J. Kotlikoff, "Deficit Delusion," *Public Interest* 84 (1986): 53–65; Laurence J. Kotlikoff, *Generational Accounting: Knowing Who Pays, and When, for What We Spend* (New York: Free Press, 1992); Laurence J. Kotlikoff, "From Deficit Delusion to the Fiscal Balance Rule: Looking for an Economically Meaningful Way to Assess Fiscal Policy," *Journal of Economics* 58, no. 1 (1993): 17–41; and Alan J. Auerbach and Laurence J. Kotlikoff, *Dynamic Fiscal Policy* (Cambridge: Cambridge University Press, 1987). An important theme in this literature is that fiscal imbalances typically imply large redistributions across generations, with future generations facing substantially higher taxes to pay for the retirement and health benefits of existing retirees. I abstract from these issues here. For an excellent discussion, see Alan J. Auerbach, Jagadeesh Gokhale, and Laurence J. Kotlikoff, "Generational Accounting: A Meaningful Way to Evaluate Fiscal Policy," *Journal of Economic Perspectives* (1994): 73–94.

[12] As an aside, this is also why balanced budget amendments are a problematic way to reduce the size of government.

13

The deficit is also an incomplete measure of fiscal imbalance because it fails to account for the future expenditures and revenues implied by current policies. An economy with current deficits can be in balance if current policies imply declining expenditure or increasing taxes. Alternately, an economy with current surpluses can be imbalanced if current policies imply rising expenditure or falling taxes. Similarly, the implication of even persistent deficits depends on an economy's growth prospects: a healthy economy can generate the tax revenue to pay off deficits; a sick one cannot.

As illustration, consider the history of U.S. federal deficits, displayed in Figure 1. Deficits were small before the Great Depression, rarely exceeding 1–2 percent of GDP except during the Civil War and World War I. Deficits grew during the early 1930s and soared during World War II but returned to modest levels for several decades. Deficits then escalated during the 1970s and 1980s before shrinking and turning to surplus in the 1990s. Substantial deficits returned during the financial crisis and Great Recession, but deficits have since moved back toward historical norms. Thus, the U.S. federal deficit displays little consistent long-run trend. Over this period, however, the size and scope of government have increased dramatically, so the path of the deficit gives only the vaguest hint of the fundamental change in the role of government in the United States.

Figure 1

U.S. Deficit as a Percentage of GDP, 1792–2014

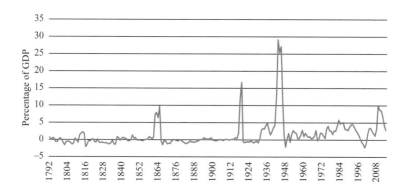

Source: Generated by the author using historical deficit data from http://www.usgovernmentspending.com/.

Figure 2
U.S. DEBT AS A PERCENTAGE OF GDP, 1792–2014

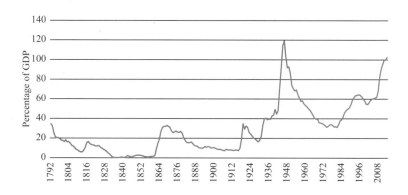

SOURCE: Generated by the author using historical debt data from
http://www.usgovernmentspending.com/.

The outstanding debt suffers similar limitations as a measure of government's financial situation. The debt is backward looking; it takes no account of what current policy implies for future expenditures or revenue. Any surplus reduces the debt, and any deficit increases the debt, regardless of whether that deficit or surplus consists of high expenditure and high revenues or low expenditure and low revenues. Similarly, whether a given ratio of debt to output is problematic depends on an economy's growth prospects.

Consider, as illustration, the history of debt relative to GDP in the United States, displayed in Figure 2. Debt rose during each major war (1812, Civil War, World War I, World War II) but then declined quickly afterwards. During WWII, debt rose dramatically, to over 100 percent of GDP, but within two decades had fallen to less than 40 percent.[13] High debt was not cause for great alarm at the end of these wars because the

---

[13] Consistent with the analysis above, the apparent improvement in the debt from the 1960s onward masks a gradual but consistent increase in unfunded liabilities that exceeded the reduction in explicit liabilities. Thus, fiscal balance was getting worse despite the fall in the debt. See "U.S. Fiscal Imbalance over Time: This Time *Is* Different," the second essay in this volume.

expenditure that caused the increased debt was temporary and because the economy's growth path was good.[14]

As further illustration, consider the debt ratios of European countries in 2007, the year before the onset of the worldwide financial crisis.[15] Greece's ratio was 112.8 percent, and Italy's was 110.6 percent, consistent with high debt ratios tending to predict slower growth and fiscal difficulties. Yet the ratios for other countries that experienced such difficulties were smaller, with Spain at 41.7 percent, Ireland at 27.5 percent, and Portugal at 78.1 percent. Additionally, several countries that avoided fiscal crises had relatively high debt ratios in 2007, with the United States at 75.7 percent, Canada at 84.3 percent, Belgium at 93.6 percent, and Japan at 177 percent. These examples do not mean debt plays no role in fiscal imbalance, but they illustrate that the debt is only one component of the complete picture and therefore a noisy predictor of fiscal difficulties.

The deficit and the debt are thus components of a government's fiscal imbalance, but for most economies, they are incomplete and therefore inaccurate measures of fiscal imbalance. Large and persistent deficits do imply a growing debt-to-GDP ratio, and persistently high and growing debt is associated with slower growth and fiscal difficulties.[16] But over a broad range, a government's debt or deficit can be large or small without significant implications for government's overall fiscal health.

Calculating Fiscal Imbalance

Since neither the debt nor the deficit provides accurate information on whether a government's expenditure and revenue plans are sustain-

---

[14] Inflation also helped reduce the debt-to-GDP ratio after WWII; see Joshua Aizenman and Nancy Marion, "Using Inflation to Erode the U.S. Public Debt," NBER Working Paper no. 15562, December 2009.

[15] Data sourced from the "General Government Debt [indicator]," Organisation for Economic Co-operation and Development, 2015, doi:10.1787/a0528cc2-en.

[16] See especially Carmen M. Reinhart and Kenneth S. Rogoff, "Growth in a Time of Debt," *American Economic Review* 100, no. 2 (2010): 573–78; and Carmen M. Reinhart, Vincent R. Reinhart, and Kenneth S. Rogoff, "Public Debt Overhangs: Advanced-Economy Episodes Since 1800," *Journal of Economic Perspectives* 26, no. 3 (2012): 69–86. Subsequent work attacked the Reinhart and Rogoff conclusion; see Thomas Herndon, Michael Ash, and Robert Pollin, "Does High Public Debt Consistently Stifle Economic Growth? A Critique of Reinhart and Rogoff," *Cambridge Journal of Economics* 38, no. 2 (2014): 257–79. Reinhart and Rogoff subsequently showed that their results are robust to these criticisms; see Carmen M. Reinhart and Kenneth S. Rogoff, "Debt, Growth and the Austerity Debate," *New York Times*, op-ed, April 25, 2013, as well as the further documentation discussed there.

able, a different approach is necessary. This approach must consider the entire path of future expenditure and revenue, in addition to the existing debt. The key question is how to "add up" expenditures and revenues in different time periods. This section addresses this issue under the assumption that government can project the expenditure and revenue from its existing policies with certainty. This assumption is unrealistic, but it allows the simplest presentation of key issues. I discuss the implications of uncertainty in the Appendix.

Consider first an economy that exists for exactly one year. For simplicity, I assume in the derivations below that this government has zero initial debt; fiscal imbalance calculations for actual economies would add existing explicit debt to these formulas. So, the government's fiscal imbalance equals its expenditure minus its revenues in that year.[17] The magnitude of the imbalance indicates how much additional revenue the government must raise to afford its current expenditure.

Next consider an economy that lasts two years. The government has planned expenditure and projected revenues in each year, but expenditure might exceed or fall short of revenue in either year. What is this government's fiscal imbalance?

The naïve answer is that imbalance equals the sum of the government's expenditure over the two years minus the sum of its revenues over the two years. This ignores, however, that revenues might not equal expenditure in either year, even if total revenue over the two years equals total expenditure over the two years. If expenditure exceeds revenue in the first period, the government must borrow; so the required revenue exceeds the sum of the expenditure amounts by the interest payments on the debt for the one year of borrowing. If expenditure is less than revenue in the first year, the government can lend the surplus; so the required revenue falls short of total expenditure by the interest earned on government saving for the one year of saving.

Calculations of fiscal imbalance, therefore, require the concept of present value. This is an approach to adding up cash flows over time

---

[17] An interesting question is whether fiscal imbalance should account for the value of government assets like land, mineral rights, timber, and more. Although such assets might have substantial value (according to one estimate, more than $150 trillion; see the Institute for Energy Research's website at http://instituteforenergyresearch.org /analysis/federal-assets-above-and-below-ground/), they should mainly not be included in fiscal imbalance. The reason is that fiscal imbalance is about expenditure and revenue under current policy, and these government assets add only modest revenue.

that accounts for the fact that, when borrowing and lending are possible, a dollar today has a different value than a dollar in the future (assuming a non-zero interest rate). In particular, the value today—to any economic entity, whether an individual, business, or government—of a dollar one year from now is

$$1 / (1 + r),$$

where r is the rate at which this economic entity can lend. The reasoning is that if this entity has

$$1 / (1 + r)$$

dollars now, and lends it out for one year at the interest rate r, then this amount will grow to

$$[1 / (1 + r)] * (1 + r) = 1$$

over one year. By extension, the value today of a dollar two years from now is

$$1 / [(1 + r) * (1 + r)],$$

since that amount invested for two years will grow to one dollar by the end of the second year. Thus, a rational economic entity should be indifferent between getting the "discounted" amount today or getting one dollar exactly two years from today, given the interest rate r. The same reasoning applies for cash flows T periods in the future; the value now of receiving a dollar T years in the future is

$$1 / (1 + r)^T.$$

This reasoning applies to any cash outflow or inflow and so applies identically to expenditure or revenue.

Applying this approach to a hypothetical economy that lasts two years, fiscal imbalance is the present value of expenditure minus the present value of revenues over two years, or

$$\text{Fiscal Imbalance} = (\text{Exp}_1 + \text{Exp}_2 / (1 + r)) - (\text{Rev}_1 + \text{Rev}_2 / (1 + r)), \quad (1)$$

where Exp stands for expenditure, Rev stands for revenue, and the subscripts indicate year. Equivalently, fiscal imbalance is the present value of current and future primary deficits (i.e., the deficit excluding interest payments on the debt).

If the amount in Equation (1) is greater than zero (the present value of expenditure exceeds the present value of revenue), then government is fiscally imbalanced, and the magnitude of the fiscal imbalance indicates how much additional revenue the government must raise (in present value) to pay for its expenditure over time. Equivalently, fiscal imbalance indicates how much the government would have to cut expenditure (in present value) to avoid raising taxes. If the amount in Equation (1) is zero or negative (the present value of expenditure is less than the present value of revenues), then this government is in fiscal balance and can carry out its planned expenditure.

To illustrate, assume an economy's policies imply expenditure of $100 in year one and $110 in year two, along with revenues of $110 in year one and $100 in year two; so for this economy, expenditure equals revenue over the two years, but not year-by-year. Assume the interest rate is 10 percent. Then,

$$\text{Fiscal Imbalance} = (100 + 110 \;/\; (1 + 0.10)) - (110 + 100 \;/\; (1 + 0.10)),$$
$$= (100 + 100) - (110 + 91),$$
$$= 200 - 201,$$
$$= -1.$$

This economy is balanced because the present value of expenditure is less than the present value of revenues. Alternatively, assume that expenditure is $110 in year one and $100 in year two, while revenue is $100 in year one and $110 in year two. Again, expenditure equals revenue over the two years, but again, not year-by-year and with a different pattern than above. For this economy,

$$\text{Fiscal Imbalance} = (110 + 100 \;/\; (1 + 0.10)) - (100 + 110 \;/\; (1 + 0.10)),$$
$$= (110 + 91) - (100 + 100),$$
$$= 201 - 200,$$
$$= 1.$$

This economy is fiscally imbalanced because the present value of expenditure exceeds the present value of revenues. These two hypothetical economies differ only in the timing of their expenditure and revenue, but this makes a difference for fiscal balance.

The fact that expenditure might exceed or fall short of revenue in a particular year does not indicate whether a government is in fiscal balance. For example, U.S. deficits have been declining for several years (see Figure 1), but as shown later, the United States has a substantial imbalance. Further, fiscal imbalance has been growing over this same period.[18]

---

[18] See the estimates in Jagadeesh Gokhale and Kent Smetters, *Fiscal and Generational Imbalances: New Budget Measures for New Budget Priorities* (Washington, D.C.: AEI Press, 2003); Jagadeesh Gokhale and Kent Smetters, "Fiscal and Generational Imbalances: An Update," in *Tax Policy and the Economy*, Vol. 20, ed. James M. Poterba (Cambridge, MA: MIT Press, 2006), pp. 193–223; and Jagadeesh Gokhale, "Spending Beyond Our Means: How We Are Bankrupting Future Generations," Cato Institute White Paper, 2013.

Extending the present value approach to a longer-lived but still finite-lived economy is straightforward. The present values of expenditure and revenue have as many terms as years of expenditure and revenue, with each additional term discounted by an additional factor of $(1 + r)$. For a three-period economy, for example, fiscal imbalance is

Fiscal Imbalance = $(\text{Exp}_1 + \text{Exp}_2 / (1 + r) + \text{Exp}_3 / (1 + r)^2) -$
$(\text{Rev}_1 + \text{Rev}_2 / (1 + r) + \text{Rev}_3 / (1 + r)^2)$.

The extension to any finite number of periods follows the same logic.

Real world economies, however, go on forever, so present value calculations must include an infinite number of terms.[19] The basic principle is still the same: add up all the expenditures and revenues at different periods, with each period's expenditure and revenue discounted back to the present by a discount factor that reflects the number of periods in the future at which that expenditure or revenue occurs. It might seem impossible to add up an infinite number of terms, but under reasonable assumptions, these summations simplify using standard formulas. All calculations of fiscal imbalance for the infinite future use these formulas.

The crucial question in calculating fiscal imbalance (or any present value) is what interest rate to use. This interest rate should reflect the opportunity cost of funds, meaning the interest that could be earned if those funds were lent out rather than paying for expenditure.

In the hypothetical economies considered here—with no uncertainty about the future—the choice of interest rate is trivial, since in a world of certainty, all assets must yield the same return or interest rate. If any asset offered a higher return, everyone would buy it, driving its price up and lowering its return. If any asset offered a lower return, everyone would sell it, driving its price down and raising its return. Thus, under certainty, only one interest rate exists in the marketplace, so this is (trivially) the interest rate to use in present value calculations.

In the real world, substantial uncertainty exists about the returns on different assets, so different interest rates (or, more broadly, rates of return) are available on different financial assets (e.g., stocks vs. bonds). The question is then which rate to use in an analysis that wishes to abstract from this uncertainty. Standard practice is to use a "certainty

---

[19] The extension of present value to an infinite horizon requires the additional assumption that the cash flows being discounted do not grow faster than the interest rate; if they did, the infinite sum would equal infinity.

equivalent" interest rate, meaning the rate for assets that are essentially default free. Typically, the assumed interest rate is the average yield on long-term federal government debt.[20] This approach is reasonable, but since this interest rate varies significantly over time, nontrivial uncertainty still exists over exactly which rate to use.

A related question is whether to discount future expenditures and revenues at a real or nominal interest rate. The answer is that present value calculations should discount real projections at a real rate and nominal projections at a nominal rate. Assuming the same inflation rate is used to convert the interest rate from nominal to real as is used to adjust future cash flows for inflation, these two approaches give identical answers.

Beyond these general questions about what interest rate to use in fiscal imbalance calculations, a crucial point is that the choice of interest rate matters, potentially a great deal. At one extreme, using an interest rate of zero means that the present value of a sequence of cash flows just equals the sum of all these flows. At the other extreme, a large interest rate makes most terms other than the first few irrelevant, because dividing them by one plus the interest rate raised to a large power makes the discounted value close to zero. In that case, present value reflects the first few terms, and flows at longer horizons hardly matter.

Just as important, moderate differences in the chosen interest rate (e.g., 3 percent vs. 4 percent) have a surprisingly large impact on the value of fiscal imbalance. For example, the value of one (inflation adjusted) dollar per year from now to infinity is $34.33 when the (real) interest rate is 3 percent but $26.00 when the (real) interest rate is 4 percent. Since the exact choice of interest rate is never unambiguous, this choice introduces nontrivial uncertainty about the magnitude of fiscal imbalance.

Another important fact about fiscal imbalance is that reducing it sooner is better than reducing it later, since any imbalance grows at the rate of interest. The magnitude of expenditure reduction or tax increase necessary to achieve fiscal balance increases with each year in which

---

[20] For example, see Gokhale, "Spending Beyond Our Means," note 15: "The discount rate applied to calculate present values equals the interest rate on the government's longest-maturity (30 year) Treasury securities. That current rate turns out to be very close to the discount rate used in earlier fiscal and generational accounting estimates of 3.67 percent."

no adjustment in policy occurs, and such increases accumulate over time. In particular, imbalance will normally grow relative to GDP in the absence of changes in tax or expenditure policy.[21] If, for example, the interest rate the government pays to borrow is 3 percent and the economy's growth rate is 2 percent, the imbalance relative to GDP doubles in roughly 75 years.[22]

A final point about fiscal imbalance is that the present value approach is related to graphs of the projected ratio of explicit debt to GDP, such as those presented in the Congressional Budget Office's (CBO) *Long-Term Budget Outlook*.[23] Figure 3 reproduces an example from the most recent *Outlook*. This graph shows the projected ratio of debt to GDP, 75 years into the future, based on assumed expenditure and revenue paths and an assumed interest rate. Such graphs rely on data similar to those in present

Figure 3

CBO PROJECTIONS OF DEBT RELATIVE TO GDP

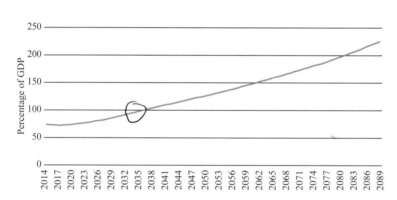

SOURCE: CBO, *The 2015 Long-Term Budget Outlook.*

[21] This follows because the interest rate r is normally greater than the growth rate of GDP.

[22] This follows from the Rule of 72, which states that at an interest rate of r percent, it takes $72/r$ years for an initial amount to double. For further explanation, see Zvi Bodie, Alan Marcus, and Alex Kane, *Investments*, 10th ed. (New York: McGraw Hill Education, 2014).

[23] Congressional Budget Office, *The 2015 Long-Term Budget Outlook* (June 2015), https://www.cbo.gov/sites/default/files/114th-congress-2015-2016/reports/50250 -LongTermBudgetOutlook-4.pdf.

value calculations. A graph that shows an upward trending path for debt relative to GDP is equivalent to fiscal imbalance, and vice versa.[24]

Estimates of Fiscal Imbalance

Given the present value framework for measuring fiscal imbalance, how large are the fiscal imbalances in the United States and Europe?

Table 1 summarizes recent estimates of fiscal imbalance.[25] Each entry gives the estimated value of fiscal imbalance—explicit debt plus the implicit debt implied by continuation of current policies into the future—relative to the present value of future GDP. These estimates are for 2012 (United States) and 2010 (Europe). In most cases, updated estimates would be larger since these countries have not made major adjustments to their expenditure or tax policies and have been running significant deficits over the past several years.

For the United States, the estimated fiscal imbalance is 5.4 percent of the present value of GDP under the CBO's baseline projections of future expenditure and revenue and 9.0 percent under its alternative projections. CBO's alternative scenario assumes that certain policy changes that have occurred regularly in the past, such as adjustment of the Alternative Minimum Tax for inflation, will continue to occur in the future. This is arguably a better representation of "continuing current policy" than the baseline representation, which assumes policymakers will not make such regular adjustments.[26, 27]

---

[24] The only difference between the present value calculation and the graphical analysis is that the graph does not explicitly account for what happens beyond the time horizon of the graph, while a present value calculation for the entire future would. For this reason, the present value approach might appear more complete. Any calculations for expenditure and revenue in the infinite future, however, are based on assumptions that these will grow at some constant rate based on historical experience or other factors. These same assumptions are implicit in the graphical presentation. Thus, the two approaches are equivalent for all practical purposes.

[25] Gokhale, "Spending Beyond Our Means," Tables 6 and 7; and Jagadeesh Gokhale, "The Government Debt Iceberg," Table 12, *Institute of Economic Affairs Monographs, Research Monograph* 68 (2014). These estimates update earlier ones in Gokhale and Smetters, *Fiscal and Generational Imbalances: New Budget Measures*; and Gokhale and Smetters, "Fiscal and Generational Imbalances: An Update."

[26] CBO, *The 2015 Long-Term Budget Outlook.*

[27] The federal government incurs implicit liabilities for policies other than explicit expenditure programs, especially loan (housing) or other guarantees, bailouts, deposit insurance, and so on. These are even more difficult to value than explicit expenditure, so I omit them here. Some implicit liabilities are very small in magnitude, so the omission is not quantitatively important. Others are not trivial but are still omitted. See James D.

Table 1
ESTIMATES OF FISCAL IMBALANCE FOR THE UNITED STATES AND
EUROPE (PERCENT OF PRESENT VALUE OF GDP)

Country	Year	Fiscal Imbalance
United States[a]	2012	5.4
United States[b]	2012	9.0
Belgium	2010	8.6
Denmark	2010	8.1
France	2010	14.6
Germany	2010	13.9
Greece	2010	17.8
Italy	2010	12.1
Netherlands	2010	11.7
Portugal	2010	15.1
Spain	2010	15.4
Sweden	2010	6.8
United Kingdom	2010	13.7

[a] CBO baseline scenario.
[b] CBO alternative scenario.

For major European countries, the estimated fiscal imbalances vary significantly, but most are in double digits and most are above that of the United States—under both the baseline and alternative CBO scenarios. The differences across countries do not line up tightly with those normally thought of as being in good vs. bad fiscal condition. Greece's estimated imbalance is large, for example, but not much greater than the imbalance for Germany or the United Kingdom.

One way to put these imbalances in perspective is to ask how much taxes would have to rise to restore fiscal balance. In the United States, the estimated imbalance amounts to 25.5 percent of total federal receipts under CBO's baseline assumptions and 50.3 percent under CBO's alter-

Hamilton, "Off-Balance-Sheet Federal Liabilities," NBER Working Paper no. w19253, July 2013; Charles W. Calomiris, "Financial Innovation, Regulation, and Reform," *Cato Journal* 29 (2009): 65; and Philip Swagel, "Off-Balance-Sheet Federal Liabilities: Comment," *Cato Papers on Public Policy* 3 (2014): 45–54.

Figure 4

CBO PROJECTIONS OF FEDERAL EXPENDITURE SHARES,
BASELINE ASSUMPTIONS

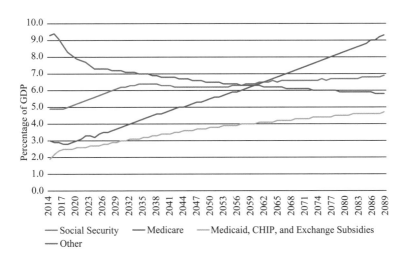

── Social Security ── Medicare ──Medicaid, CHIP, and Exchange Subsidies
── Other

SOURCE: CBO, *The 2015 Long-Term Budget Outlook.*

native assumptions.[28] In Europe, total government tax revenues would have to rise 29.9 percent from current levels.[29]

A crucial question about these imbalances is which components of expenditure contribute most significantly. This is different than asking which programs are balanced on their own; as discussed, that question is not well defined because governments can use any tax revenues to make any kind of expenditure. But it is entirely legitimate to ask which programs generate the expenditure that contributes to a rising imbalance between total expenditure and revenues in the projections that underlie fiscal imbalance estimates.

Figures 4 and 5 display the baseline and alternative CBO projections of the major components of federal spending relative to GDP over the next 75 years.[30] These projections show that imbalance is mainly about the path of spending on the federal government's major health care pro-

---

[28] See Gokhale, "Spending Beyond Our Means," Table 10, p. 16.
[29] See Gokhale, "The Government Debt Iceberg," Table 14, p. 123.
[30] CBO, *The 2015 Long-Term Budget Outlook.*

Figure 5

CBO PROJECTIONS OF FEDERAL EXPENDITURE SHARES, ALTERNATIVE
ASSUMPTIONS

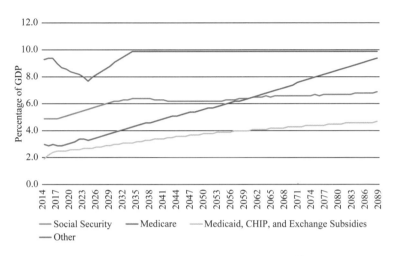

SOURCE: CBO, *The 2015 Long-Term Budget Outlook.*

grams (Medicare, Medicaid, the Children's Health Insurance Program, and the Affordable Care Act) and, to a lesser degree, Social Security. A similar conclusion applies in Europe, although retirement spending accounts for a higher share of overall expenditure on the elderly.

One possible caveat about these imbalance estimates is that, since the early 2000s, health care cost inflation has moderated substantially in the United States. The reasons for this slowdown are not fully understood, but they predate the recession and the Affordable Care Act, so those two factors are—at a minimum—not the whole story. If this slowdown continues over the long haul, it will moderate the growth in government health care expenditure and therefore imply smaller estimates of fiscal imbalance.[31]

For several reasons, however, this "good news" should be taken with a grain of salt. Health care cost inflation slowed in the early 1990s but then accelerated again. Some of the excess growth of federal health-related expenditure reflects demographics rather than just health care

[31] See Amitabh Chandra, Jonathan Holmes, and Jonathan Skinner, "Is This Time Different? The Slowdown in Health Care Spending," *Brookings Papers on Economic Activity,* Fall 2013, pp. 261–311.

cost inflation; as baby boomers retire and life expectancy increases, the fraction of the population receiving Medicare will continue to grow faster than the economy even with less health care cost inflation. And projections that incorporate less rapid health care cost inflation still show Medicare and other health-related expenditure growing faster than GDP by enough to make the imbalance large.[32]

Policy Options

If the projections underlying recent estimates of fiscal imbalance are accurate, countries that do nothing to reduce these imbalances will likely face fiscal crises. This follows because any given imbalance increases at the interest rate on government borrowing. Any imbalance will eventually become so large, therefore, that lenders either refuse to roll over a country's debt or demand ever higher interest rates, which makes the imbalance worse.

That does not mean the United States and the major European economies face imminent crisis; the day of reckoning may be many years or decades away. Evidently, markets trust that the world's major economies will make appropriate adjustments before a Greek-style fiscal crisis occurs. But that trust is unlikely to last in the face of higher and higher imbalances, and predicting when markets will change their minds is difficult. Thus, prudent countries should reduce their imbalances sooner rather than later.

Countries in fiscal imbalance have three options for avoiding fiscal meltdown: stimulate economic growth (because this increases revenue and reduces some kinds of expenditure), raise taxes (including possibly the inflation tax), or reduce spending. I address each of these in turn.

Adopting policies that spur growth is always desirable, and all countries have innumerable opportunities to do so. Even absent political obstacles, however, the degree to which better policies can promote growth has limits; fiscal balance estimates already assume growth rates that may be too optimistic given the slow growth rates in the United States and Europe since the Great Recession. Thus, while improved growth policies are an excellent complement to other adjustments, they will likely not solve fiscal imbalance problems by themselves.

---

[32] See Douglas Elmendorf, "Comment," *Brookings Papers on Economic Activity*, Fall 2013, pp. 311–19.

Raising taxes reduces fiscal imbalances, other things held constant. But higher taxes also reduce economic growth, and that offsets some of the reduced imbalance. At low initial tax rates, the net impact is reduced imbalance; but as rates climb, the net impact declines and eventually becomes perverse: high tax rates generate less revenue (the Laffer curve). In particular, beyond some level of fiscal imbalance, tax increases can never restore balance because higher rates generate lower revenue as well as higher expenditure on programs like unemployment or disability insurance.

Whether the United States and Europe can achieve balance solely via higher taxes is unclear. My own hunch is that this is close to impossible in the United States and utterly impossible in Europe. Average tax burdens are already much higher there than here, implying many European countries are close to (or already on) the wrong side of the Laffer curve. The political obstacles to higher taxes are also likely substantial.

One specific "tax" that countries might employ to reduce fiscal imbalance is higher inflation. That would erode the inflation-adjusted value of those expenditures whose real value declines with inflation, such as repayment of nominal debt. Whether inflation erodes the inflation-adjusted value of other expenditures is less clear, since many of these are either explicitly indexed to inflation (e.g., Social Security benefits) or implicitly indexed to inflation via the political process (e.g., Medicare expenditures, assuming the federal government increases reimbursements to health care providers by at least the inflation rate). In addition, higher inflation faces substantial political opposition and under some circumstances can impose significant costs on the economy. Thus, modestly higher inflation could reduce fiscal imbalance to some degree but is unlikely to eliminate imbalance by itself.

Cutting expenditure also reduces imbalances, other things held constant, but the overall impact depends on the kind of expenditure and the circumstances. In the Keynesian model, the direct benefit of expenditure reductions might be offset by lower tax revenues due to slower growth. This is a short-run effect, however; so again the changes in expenditure motivated by Keynesian stabilization concerns have minimal implication for fiscal imbalance. Reducing expenditure on those programs that are necessary for economic growth is likely counter-productive even though the direct impact is to reduce fiscal imbalance.

That leaves only one plausible avenue for substantially reducing fiscal imbalance: cutting expenditure on programs that either harm or have minimal impact on economic productivity and growth. Reducing or eliminating such programs is a win-win, since both the direct impact and any indirect impact in promoting growth reduce fiscal imbalance.

The list of productivity-damaging programs is long and varied, but the expenditure accounted for by many of these programs is trivial relative to the magnitude of fiscal imbalance (e.g., agricultural subsidies or the Export-Import Bank). Thus even killing off dozens or hundreds of such programs would not make a noticeable difference.

A substantial reduction in fiscal imbalance is therefore likely to require significant cuts (relative to existing projections) in Medicare, Medicaid, and Obamacare. While these programs can have efficiency benefits under some conditions, their main impact is to redistribute resources rather than promote economic efficiency. Indeed, these programs potentially generate substantial efficiency losses, both from the distortions caused by the taxation necessary to fund them and from the adverse incentives these programs create for saving and labor supply.[33] Plausibly the most attractive way to reduce expenditure on these programs is to expand cost sharing substantially via higher copayments and deductibles. Such changes would reduce expenditure directly, and with greater "skin-in-the-game," patients would be more price-sensitive and more likely purchase less health care. That would reduce health care cost inflation and thereby expenditure.

The political feasibility of major cuts in government health care spending is problematic. Nevertheless, such reductions are crucial for achieving major improvements in fiscal balance because, while other expenditure programs are large (e.g., national defense), they are not growing ever larger as a share of GDP. Even substantial reductions in those other programs would be "one-offs." Such cuts would lower deficits initially, but if health care expenditures perpetually grow faster than GDP, those cuts would not slow the growth in deficits long term.

---

[33] See, for example, Aaron Yellowitz, "The Medicaid Notch, Labor Supply, and Welfare Participation: Evidence from Eligibility Expansions," *Quarterly Journal of Economics* 110 (1995): 909–39; Aaron Yellowitz and Jonathan Gruber, "Public Health Insurance and Private Savings," *Journal of Political Economy* 107 (1999): 1249–74; R. Glenn Hubbard, Jonathan Skinner, and Stephen P. Zeldes, "Precautionary Saving and Social Insurance," *Journal of Political Economy* 103 (1995): 360–99; and Casey B. Mulligan, *Side Effects: The Economic Consequences of Health Reform* (Floosmoor, IL: JMJ Economics, 2014).

Conclusions

The discussion above makes several points, which are summarized here.

Measuring fiscal imbalance is different from evaluating individual programs. Any program can be imbalanced but desirable or balanced but undesirable. Fiscal imbalance is also different from Keynesian fiscal stimulus. Such a stimulus normally worsens fiscal imbalance but is temporary and therefore has minor impact on imbalance. Fiscal imbalance is about the sustainability of government programs over the long term; it answers the question, "How much extra revenue would have to be raised (in present value) to afford the expenditure planned under current policy?"

Being in fiscal balance does not mean an economy's overall level of expenditure, or its expenditure on any particular program, is desirable; balance merely indicates that the path of total expenditure is affordable. Conversely, fiscal imbalance does not indicate which policies are undesirable; imbalance just means that the path of total expenditure is not affordable.

Whether a given fiscal imbalance can be addressed via higher taxes depends on the degree to which taxes lower growth. If the impact is too large, then balance can be restored only via expenditure reductions. The main drivers of imbalance are the projected growth of government expenditure on health care and retirement programs. Recent reductions in health care cost inflation have moderated imbalances relative to earlier projections, but these imbalances are still large and growing.

Reasonable people can disagree on exactly how the world's major economies should reduce their fiscal imbalances, but no one should dispute the value of the fiscal balance perspective, nor the need to take action as soon as possible. The fundamental economic reality implied by fiscal imbalances is that the "rich" economies are not as rich as they would like to believe; they are planning far more expenditure than they can afford. Recognizing this fact sooner rather than later does not eliminate the problem, but it allows for more balanced, rational, and ultimately less costly adjustments. And if attention to fiscal imbalance helps cut ill-advised expenditure, economies can have their cake and eat it too.

Appendix: Fiscal Imbalance with Uncertainty

The discussion above, and much of the literature on fiscal imbalance, treats future expenditure and revenues as known with certainty. In real economies, government expenditure and revenue are uncertain because they depend on future output, employment, immigration, wages, prices, demographics, and the like, which are themselves uncertain. A recession, for example, means greater expenditure for policies like unemployment or disability insurance, along with decreased tax revenue. Worse, unexpectedly higher expenditure and lower revenue often occur simultaneously.

Estimates of fiscal balance take one of three approaches to dealing with uncertainty about future expenditure and revenues. The first is to ignore the issue. That means treating forecasts of future expenditure and revenue as certain and discounting those flows at a "certainty-equivalent" interest rate, meaning the rate for assets that are essentially default free. As noted in the preceding discussion, the assumed interest rate is typically the average yield on long-term federal government debt.[34]

A second approach to uncertainty estimates imbalance for a range of forecasts about future expenditure and revenue, but still discounts at a certainty-equivalent interest rate. This modification provides a sense of how different assumptions about long-run economic or demographic variables might affect fiscal balance.

Both standard approaches to uncertainty provide useful benchmarks, but each is incomplete. Most fundamentally, uncertainty necessitates making a choice about which interest rate to use in present value calculations because, when significant uncertainty exists, different assets pay substantially different rates on average as compensation for the variability of those returns.

The third approach to uncertainty therefore adjusts the interest rate used to discount future cash flows, rather than adjusting the forecasts of expenditure and revenue. This method derives from the standard principles of financial economics, which hold that uncertain future flows should be discounted at an interest rate that reflects the kind and degree of uncertainty about these flows.[35] Roughly, more uncertainty means a

---

[34] See footnote 20.

[35] See, for example, Bodie, Marcus, and Kane, *Investments*.

greater chance of "bad" outcomes, which means these flows should be treated as less likely to occur.

More precisely, and as applied in the context here, the interest rate should reflect the correlation between the cash flow in question and the economy's growth rate. That is because the growth rate affects the amount of tax revenue and, therefore, the government's ability to make the expenditure without extra borrowing or higher taxes. If expenditure tends to be high when the economy's growth rate is good (and thus tax revenues are elevated), the government will have little difficulty making the expenditure and so can "discount" the expenditure more; that is, it should use a high interest rate. If expenditure tends to be high when the economy's growth rate is low (and thus tax revenues are low), then the government will face greater difficulty making the expenditure and so should not discount the expenditure heavily; that is, it should use a low interest rate.

Some types of government expenditure are negatively correlated with the economy's growth rate, such as Medicaid, Medicare, and unemployment or disability insurance. Other components are potentially positively correlated, such as Social Security (which is indexed to wages) or highway spending. Thus, adjustment for uncertainty can go in either direction overall.

At this point, the practical importance of adjustments for uncertainty is unclear, since much of the literature does not address the issue. Some recent research has estimated adjustments for the value of Social Security benefits, with the weight of the evidence suggesting that adjusting for uncertainty reduces the future liability by a substantial but not enormous amount.[36, 37] Future work might indicate that existing imbalance

---

[36] John Geanakoplos and Stephen P. Zeldes, "Market Valuation of Accrued Social Security Benefits," NBER Working Paper no. 15170, 2009; Alexander W. Blocker, Laurence J. Kotlikoff, and Stephen A. Ross, "The True Cost of Social Security," NBER Working Paper no. 14427, 2008; and Laurence J. Kotlikoff, "A Hidden Fiscal Crisis," *Finance & Development* 47, no. 3 (2010): 30–33.

[37] For analyses of the balance in state and local government pension funds, adjusting for uncertainty appears to make a significant difference. This is because standard practice has taken a strong and likely inaccurate stand. Pursuant to Generally Accepted Accounting Principles, these governments have typically assumed that pension assets will grow at the same relatively high rate of return as portfolios that include substantial risky assets; in addition, they have assumed this rate of return justifies discounting their future liabilities at this same rate. The result implies lower discounted values for the future expenditure, making the pension funds look relatively solvent.

estimates need additional, nontrivial modifications. But since adjustments for uncertainty might suggest greater liabilities for some components and lower liabilities for others, the net impact on estimated fiscal imbalance will not necessarily be large.

For many such programs, however, the "risk" associated with the expenditure is low; the relevant city or state is legally or constitutionally obligated to make these expenditures. See Jeffrey R. Brown and David W. Wilcox, "Discounting State and Local Pension Liabilities," *American Economic Review* (2009): 538–42. Even when making other government expenditures is difficult (implying a need for higher taxes), pension expenditures must still be made. That means these funds should not be discounted at the uncertainty-adjusted interest rate but at a "certainty" rate such as that on municipal debt or treasury bonds. That implies substantially higher values for implicit pension liabilities. See Novy-Marx and Rauh, "Public Pension Promises."

U.S. Fiscal Imbalance over Time: This Time *Is* Different

Jeffrey Miron

Department of Economics, Harvard University, and the Cato Institute

Executive Summary

The U.S. fiscal imbalance—the excess of what we expect to spend, including repayment of our debt, over what government expects to receive in revenue—is large and growing. And with politicians proposing large new expenditures, little is being done to rectify the country's fiscal health. Although some policymakers argue that fiscal meltdowns have never happened in U.S. history and that therefore "this time is no different," the reality is that the nation's fiscal situation has been deteriorating since the mid-1960s, is far worse than ever before, and could lead to a fiscal crisis if no major spending adjustments occur in the next few decades.

To demonstrate this argument, this paper projects fiscal imbalance as of every year between 1965 and 2014, using data-supported assumptions about gross domestic product (GDP) growth, revenue, and trends in mandatory spending on Social Security, Medicare, Medicaid, and other programs. The projections reveal that the United States has faced a growing fiscal imbalance since the early 1970s, largely as a consequence of continuous growth in mandatory spending. As of 2014, the fiscal imbalance stands at $117.9 trillion, with few signs of future improvement even if GDP growth accelerates or tax revenues increase relative to historic norms. Thus the only viable way to restore fiscal balance is to scale back mandatory spending policies, particularly on large health care programs such as Medicare, Medicaid, and the Affordable Care Act (ACA).

Introduction

The United States faces a challenging fiscal future. According to projections from the Congressional Budget Office (CBO), the debt-to-GDP ratio will hit at least 181 percent by 2090, and continue climbing thereafter, unless the nation adjusts its tax and spending policies.[1] If no policy changes occur and if the debt ratio continues on its projected path for an extended period, the United States will eventually face rising interest rates on its debt, an even steeper debt path, and a fiscal crisis. This outcome is not inevitable; the United States likely has decades to adjust its policies. Few dispute, however, that unless the CBO's projections are substantially too pessimistic, the United States needs major adjustments in spending or tax policies to avoid fiscal meltdown.

Despite widespread agreement that spending or tax policies must change, however, appropriate adjustments have so far not occurred. Indeed, many recent policy changes have worsened the U.S. fiscal situation. These changes include the creation of Medicare Part D ($65 billion in 2014), new subsidies under the Affordable Care Act ($13.7 billion in 2014), the expansion of Medicaid under the ACA (from $250.9 billion in 2009 to $301.5 billion in 2014), higher defense spending (from $348.46 billion in 2002 to $603.46 billion in 2014), increased spending on veterans' benefits and services (from $70.4 billion in 2006 to $161.2 billion in 2014), and greater spending on energy programs (average annual spending was $0.52 billion over 1998–2002 but $11.43 billion over 2010–2014).[2, 3]

Politicians across the spectrum, moreover, propose additional spending all the time. President Barack Obama's 2015 budget proposal, for instance, included an extra $38 billion in defense spending and a $478 billion plan to revamp the nation's roads, bridges, and ports over the next six years.[4] House Republicans responded with their own plan to set aside

---

[1] The 181 percent figure is for CBO's baseline scenario. Under CBO's alternative scenario, the ratio hits 250 percent by 2055 and is not calculated beyond that year. Congressional Budget Office, *The 2015 Long-Term Budget Outlook*, CBO-45308 (Washington, D.C., 2015), https://www.cbo.gov/publication/45308.

[2] All figures in this paragraph are nominal.

[3] For spending increases associated with Medicaid, see Medicare Payment Advisory Commission, *Status Report on Part D* (Washington, D.C., 2014), http://www.medpac.gov/documents/reports/mar14_ch14.pdf?sfvrsn=0. For all other spending increases, refer to Office of Management and Budget, *Historical Tables* (Washington, D.C., 2015), https://www.whitehouse.gov/sites/default/files/omb/budget/fy2016/assets/hist.pdf.

[4] Office of Management and Budget, *Fiscal Year 2016 Budget Overview* (Washington, D.C.), https://www.whitehouse.gov/omb/overview.

over $90 billion—tens of billions more than the White House originally requested—for a war account known as the Overseas Operations Contingency Fund, thus alleging a need for even greater defense spending.[5] Elsewhere, Democratic presidential candidate Hillary Clinton has proposed to increase federal spending by $350 billion over 10 years to help undergraduates afford tuition at public colleges without needing loans.[6] Republican Senate Majority Leader Mitch McConnell has advocated boosting highway funding by about $47 billion over the next six years.[7]

A plausible reason for America's failure to address its fiscal imbalance—the excess of what we expect to spend, including repayment of our debt, over what government expects to receive in revenue—is a belief that "this time is no different" than earlier alarms about fiscal meltdown, which have so far not occurred. In the 1980s, for example, the government experienced a large buildup of federal debt due to President Reagan's tax cuts and increases in military spending. Concern arose over the spiraling debt, causing Congressional budget showdowns during President Bill Clinton's first term, but ultimately no serious fiscal crisis ensued.

In 2011, fears of a U.S. government default arose during the debt-ceiling crisis.[8] Disagreements between members of Congress resulted in a political stalemate, massive public apprehension, and a one-notch downgrade of the U.S. credit rating.[9] Just before the deadline, however, the Budget Control Act was signed into law, raising the debt ceiling by

---

[5] Tom Howell, "Republican Budget Proposals a Tough Sell within Increasingly Polarized GOP," *Washington Times*, March 19, 2015, http://www.washingtontimes.com/news/2015/mar/19/republican-budget-proposals-a-tough-sell-within-in/?page=all.

[6] Patrick Healy, "Hillary Clinton to Offer Plan on Paying College Tuition without Needing Loans," *New York Times*, August 10, 2015, http://www.nytimes.com/2015/08/10/us/politics/hillary-clinton-to-offer-plan-on-paying-college-tuition-without-needing-loans.html.

[7] Erin Kelly, "Senate Passes U.S. Highway Funding Bill," *USA Today*, July 30, 2015, http://www.usatoday.com/story/news/2015/07/30/senate-passes-highway-funding-bill/30879319/.

[8] The United States need not have actually defaulted on its debt, at least not in the short run. Instead, it could have continued to pay interest on its debt (using ongoing revenues) so long as it cut other expenditure. See David Boaz, "Dysfunction, Default, and the Debt Ceiling Crisis," *Encyclopedia Britannica Blog*, August 1, 2011, http://blogs.britannica.com/2011/08/dysfunction-default-debt-ceiling-crisis/.

[9] Zachary Goldfarb, "S&P Downgrades U.S. Credit Rating for First Time," *Washington Post*, August 6, 2011, http://www.washingtonpost.com/business/economy/sandp-considering-first-downgrade-of-us-credit-rating/2011/08/05/gIQAqKeIxI_story.html.

over $2.1 trillion and staving off the threat of immediate default.[10] A similar crisis loomed in 2013, when Congressional inability to rein in the federal deficit almost triggered a "fiscal cliff"—a series of deep, automatic cuts to federal spending. Once again, with only hours to spare, lawmakers reached a fiscal compromise and averted larger economic consequences.[11] Overall, the past 30 years reveal a clear trend: time and time again, alarm erupts over the rising federal debt level, but full fiscal meltdown never materializes.[12]

Indeed, even amid the fiscal "close calls" over the past few years, prominent figures have argued that the growing U.S. debt level is no cause for distress. Nobel laureate economist and *New York Times* columnist Paul Krugman has stated that concerns over America's fiscal condition are far overblown, describing the "great debt panic" in the United States as "wrongheaded." [13] In a 2014 op-ed titled "The Fiscal Fizzle: An Imaginary Budget and Debt Crisis," Krugman goes on to say, "The whole thing turns out to have been a false alarm.… We don't have a debt crisis, and never did. Why did everyone important seem to think otherwise?" [14]

The Center for American Progress, a think tank, similarly argued that "long-term fiscal challenges are far less frightening than we have been led to believe" and that "debt projections start to look downright manageable" once we account for recent deficit-reduction plans and slower growth in health care costs.[15] In 2013, billionaire investor Warren Buffett cautioned against a rising debt-to-GDP ratio but remarked

[10] John Diamond and George Zodrow, *Fiscal Imbalance in the United States: Where Do We Stand?* Issue brief no. 07.23.15 (Houston, TX: Rice University, Baker Institute for Public Policy, 2015), https://bakerinstitute.org/media/files/files/6fece99e/BI-Brief-072315-TEPP_Imbalance.pdf.

[11] Matt Smith, "Obama Signs Bill Warding Off Fiscal Cliff," CNN, January 3, 2013, http://www.cnn.com/2013/01/02/politics/fiscal-cliff/.

[12] Jonathan Masters, "U.S. Deficits and the National Debt," *CFR Backgrounders* (Washington, D.C.: Council on Foreign Relations, 2012), http://www.cfr.org/united-states/us-deficits-national-debt/p27400.

[13] Paul Krugman, "Debt Is Good," *New York Times*, August 21, 2015, http://www.nytimes.com/2015/08/21/opinion/paul-krugman-debt-is-good-for-the-economy.html.

[14] Paul Krugman, "The Fiscal Fizzle: An Imaginary Budget and Debt Crisis," *New York Times*, July 20, 2014, http://www.nytimes.com/2014/07/21/opinion/Paul-Krugman-An-Imaginary-Budget-and-Debt-Crisis.html.

[15] Michael Linden and Sasha Post, *The United States' Long-Term Debt Problem Isn't as Bad as You Thought* (Washington, D.C.: Center for American Progress, 2013), https://www.americanprogress.org/issues/budget/news/2013/03/11/56048/the-united-states-long-term-debt-problem-isnt-as-bad-as-you-thought/.

that "the debt itself is not a problem" because the debt-to-GDP ratio was lower than after World War II.[16] Even U.S. Treasury Secretary Jack Lew expressed a rather positive outlook over the country's debt situation. "I don't think [our national debt] is the most pressing concern today because we have controlled the rate of growth," Secretary Lew said in testimony to Congress in June 2015. "If you look at the risks to our economy from federal spending and debt, we are in a much better position now than we were six and a half years ago.... In the next ten years, we [will] have a stable debt and deficit situation."[17]

Thus, many people dismiss claims that the federal debt is a calamity in waiting. In their view, historical patterns predict that a fiscal meltdown will not occur. Even during past periods of growing debt-to-GDP ratios, fiscal crises never materialized, so "this time is no different."

This paper argues, however, that this time *is* different: while fiscal meltdown is not imminent, the nation's fiscal situation has been deteriorating since the mid-1960s, is far worse than ever before, and will get worse as time passes and no adjustments occur.[18] The absence of past fiscal crises is no guarantee against future crises.

The paper makes this argument in three steps. First, I provide an overview of federal spending, taxation, deficits, and debt since 1792, outlining the broad trends in U.S. fiscal health over time. U.S. fiscal health has deteriorated in recent decades as measured by the debt-to-GDP ratio, but this fact alone does not suggest huge alarm. The debt is a backward-looking metric of fiscal health; it does not account for future expenditure and revenue plans. Whether the current state of fiscal health is moderately concerning or truly alarming, therefore, depends on the outlook for future expenditure and revenue.

Second, I examine the changing composition of federal expenditure during the post-1965 period. Federal expenditure has shifted in two ways: from defense toward health and retirement, and from discretion-

[16] Kate Gibson, "Buffett: U.S. Debt on Its Own 'Not a Problem,'" *MarketWatch*, January 20, 2013, http://www.marketwatch.com/story/buffett-us-debt-on-its-own-not-a-problem-2013-01-20.

[17] Susan Jones, "U.S. Treasury Secretary: $18T Debt Is 'Not the Most Pressing Concern Today,'" CNSNews.com, June 18, 2015, http://cnsnews.com/news/article/susan-jones/treasury-secretary-18t-debt-not-most-pressing-concern-today.

[18] See Congressional Budget Office, *The 2015 Long-Term Budget Outlook*, Figures 1.1 and 1.3 (Washington, D.C., 2015), https://www.cbo.gov/publication/45308. See also Alan J. Auerbach and William G. Gale, *Forgotten but Not Gone: The Long-Term Fiscal Imbalance* (Washington, D.C.: The Brookings Institution, 2014).

ary toward mandatory programs. This change in composition has created the conditions for rapidly rising future expenditure, and CBO forecasts suggest that health care spending in particular will increase substantially faster than the overall economy going forward. If those forecasts are accurate, fiscal health will decline dramatically over coming decades.

Third, I estimate the value of the U.S. fiscal imbalance as of each year from 1965 to 2014. Fiscal imbalance is a measure of fiscal health that accounts for both existing debt and future expenditures and revenues. The estimates of imbalance over time show clearly that U.S. fiscal health has been declining for several decades; such estimates also indicate how significant that deterioration has been.

The final section offers conclusions. The key policy lesson is this: to avoid a fiscal meltdown in the next few decades, the United States must slow the growth rate of federal expenditures, especially on health care. Given the magnitude of estimated imbalances, neither higher taxes nor policies to enhance growth can plausibly make a substantial difference. The good news is that reduced federal spending on health care, if carried out appropriately, can enhance the efficiency of the health care system, making such expenditure cuts a win-win for policy.

U.S. Fiscal Health over Time: A First Look

Figures 1–4 show historical data about federal expenditure, the revenue, the deficit, and the debt, all relative to GDP.

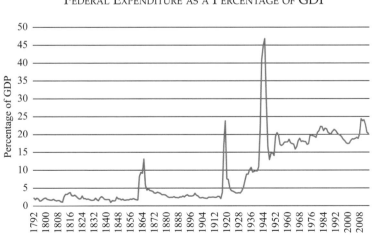

Figure 1
FEDERAL EXPENDITURE AS A PERCENTAGE OF GDP

41

Figure 1 shows that federal expenditure was less than 5 percent of GDP until the Great Depression, except during the Civil War and World War I. In the 1930s, expenditure rose to about 10 percent of GDP and then grew to over 45 percent during World War II (WWII). Expenditure declined substantially after the war but never returned to pre-Depression levels, fluctuating mainly between 15 and 20 percent of GDP but hitting almost 25 percent during the Great Recession.

Figure 2 indicates that revenue has followed a similar path to expenditure, with notable exceptions. Revenue rose less than expenditure during the Civil War, World War I, and World War II; thus, the deficit increased in each of those episodes. Revenue fluctuated between 15 and 20 percent of GDP during the post–World War II period, as did expenditure. However, revenue was lower on average, so deficits have been larger in the post-WWII period than during the peace-time portions of the pre-1929 period. Revenue dropped markedly in the early 2000s as a result of President George W. Bush's tax cuts and the 2001 recession, and it then dropped again during the Great Recession.

Consistent with the data in Figures 1–2, Figure 3 shows that the deficit was less than 1 percent of GDP (or in surplus) in most years before the 1930s, except during the War of 1812, the Civil War, and World War I. The deficit rose mildly during the Great Depression and then more noticeably during WWII, but returned to low levels in the early post-WWII period. Beginning in the 1970s and continuing through the 1980s

Figure 2
FEDERAL REVENUE AS A PERCENTAGE OF GDP

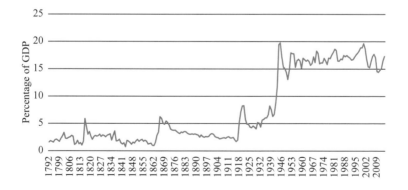

and early 1990s, deficits were typically several percent of GDP but then turned to surpluses in the last part of the century. In the 2000s deficits returned, initially as a result of the Bush tax cuts and the 2001 recession and then because of the Great Recession and higher spending under both the Bush and Obama administrations. Deficits have declined during the past few years but are still moderately high by historical standards.

Figure 4 summarizes this history of revenue and expenditure by displaying the debt-to-GDP ratio. Debt was modest by modern standards until 1929. Debt then rose during the Great Depression and WWII but fell substantially over the next several decades. Starting in the mid-1970s, expenditure outpaced revenue, so the debt grew on average, bringing the ratio to roughly 100 percent at the end of 2014.[19]

Figure 3
FEDERAL DEFICIT AS A PERCENTAGE OF GDP

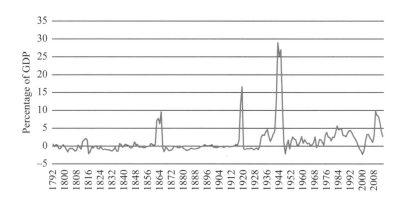

[19] This figure is for the gross debt. Net debt held by the public was 74 percent of GDP in 2014. Congressional Budget Office, *The 2015 Long-Term Budget Outlook*, CBO-50250 (Washington, D.C., 2015), https://www.usgovernmentspending.com.

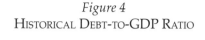

Figure 4
HISTORICAL DEBT-TO-GDP RATIO

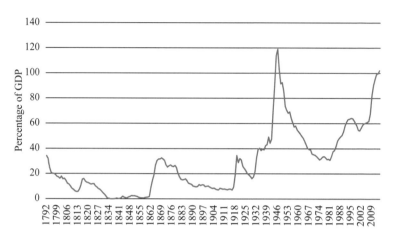

This review of U.S. fiscal history shows a deteriorating fiscal situation over the past several decades, but it does not by itself indicate whether serious concern and policy adjustment are necessary. The debt ratio, while on an upward trajectory, is no higher than at the end of WWII, after which the ratio declined for several decades. The U.S. debt ratio is also below that of other rich countries, such as the United Kingdom, France, or Japan, which have so far not experienced fiscal meltdowns. [20]

Further, the debt accounts only for past fiscal decisions, not the effects of future spending or revenue. Thus, to assess whether the current situation is cause for serious alarm, I next examine the composition of federal spending over the post-WWII period and its likely path going forward.

The Composition of Federal Spending

Figures 5–12 show annual federal expenditure for 1965–2014 for discretionary spending (total discretionary spending, defense spending,

---

[20] In 2012, gross debt over GDP was 94 percent in the United States, 97 percent in the United Kingdom, 101 percent in France, and 196 percent in Japan. See World Bank, "World Development Indicators," *World DataBank* (Washington, D.C., 2012), http://databank. worldbank.org/data/reports.aspx?Code=GC.DOD.TOTL.GD.ZS&id=af3ce82b&report_name=Popular_indicators&populartype=series&ispopular=y.

and other discretionary spending; for details see Appendix A, Table 1) as well as mandatory spending (total mandatory spending, Social Security, Medicare, Medicaid, and other mandatory spending programs; for details see Appendix B, Table 2).[21]

Figure 5 shows that total discretionary spending displays a substantial downward trend over the period, declining from roughly 10.9 percent of GDP in 1965 to only about 6.8 percent in 2014.[22] This overall reduction reflects a substantial decline in defense spending (Figure 6) combined with a modest decline in other discretionary spending (Figure 7). Defense spending averaged 8.4 percent of GDP in the 1960s, 5.6 percent in the 1970s, 5.6 percent in the 1980s, 3.8 percent in the 1990s, 3.7 percent in the 2000s, and 4.2 percent in the past four years.[23] Discretionary spending other than defense does not display a strong trend over this period but is slightly lower at the end of the sample than before.[24]

Figure 5
TOTAL DISCRETIONARY SPENDING AS A PERCENTAGE OF GDP

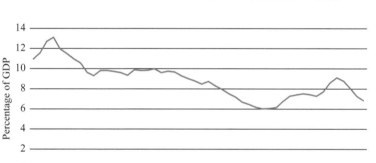

[21] "Other mandatory programs" include income security and other retirement and disability programs, as well as mandatory programs such as, but not limited to, the Medicare-Eligible Retiree Health Care Fund, the federal student loan subsidies, the Children's Health Insurance Program (CHIP), and the Affordable Care Act subsidies.

[22] Congressional Budget Office, *The Budget and Economic Outlook: 2015 to 2025*, CBO-49892 (Washington, D.C., 2015), https://www.cbo.gov/publication/49892.

[23] Office of Management and Budget, *Historical Tables* (Washington, D.C., 2015), https://www.whitehouse.gov/sites/default/files/omb/budget/fy2016/assets/hist.pdf.

[24] Ibid.

Figure 6
DEFENSE SPENDING AS A PERCENTAGE OF GDP

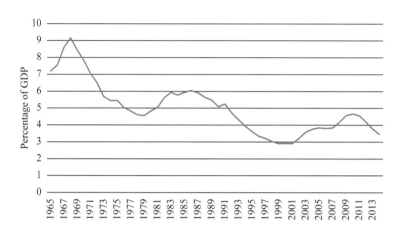

Figure 7
OTHER DISCRETIONARY SPENDING AS A PERCENTAGE OF GDP

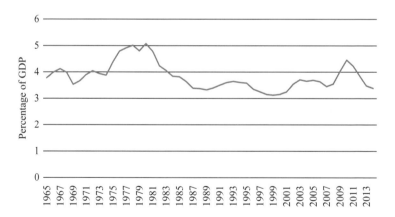

Figure 8 shows that total mandatory spending has grown from 4.5 percent of GDP in 1965 to 12.2 percent in 2014. This growth comes from three main sources. Social Security (Figure 9) has grown from 2.3 percent of GDP in 1965 to about 5 percent in recent years.[25] Spending on Medicare and Medicaid (Figures 10 and 11), which was zero until Congress created those programs in 1965, rose to 3.47 percent and 1.75 percent of GDP, respectively, by 2014.[26] Other mandatory spending (Figure 12) grew from 3.1 percent of GDP in 1965 to 3.6 percent in 2014.

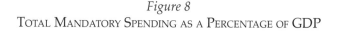

Figure 8
Total Mandatory Spending as a Percentage of GDP

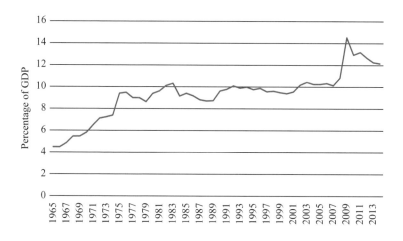

[25] Social Security taxes and lump sum payments began in 1937. However, the majority of receipts from January 1937 through December 1939 were through annual Congressional appropriations. Disbursements during the first three fiscal years of the program were exclusively lump-sum payments to the estates of deceased insured workers. Regular monthly benefits did not begin until 1940, when the Old-Age and Survivors Insurance trust fund was created and became effective. A 1941 report provides minimal information on receipts and expenditures (see the trustees report at http://www.ssa.gov/OACT/TR/historical/1941TR.html). Of about $1.75 billion in receipts of the old-age reserve account in 1937–1939, $1.31 billion was transfers from appropriations made by Congress. Over that three-year period, only $25 million was disbursed. See Social Security Administration, "FAQs," *Social Security History* (Washington, D.C.), http://www.ssa.gov/history/hfaq.html.

[26] Congressional Budget Office, *2015 Long-Term Budget Outlook*.

Figure 9
SOCIAL SECURITY SPENDING AS A PERCENTAGE OF GDP

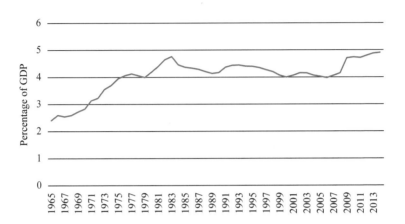

Figure 10
MEDICARE SPENDING AS A PERCENTAGE OF GDP

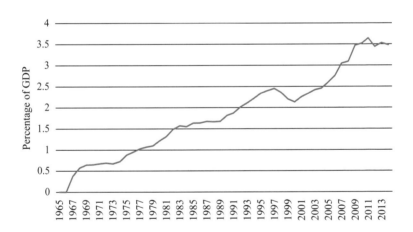

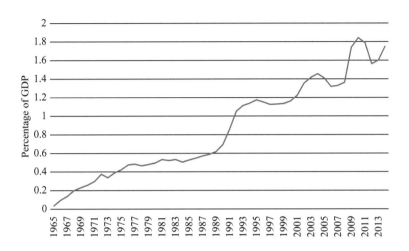

Figure 11
MEDICAID SPENDING AS A PERCENTAGE OF GDP

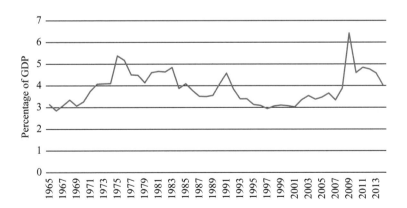

Figure 12
OTHER MANDATORY SPENDING AS A PERCENTAGE OF GDP (INCLUDING
INCOME SECURITY, OTHER RETIREMENT AND DISABILITY, OTHER PROGRAMS,
AND OTHER HEALTH PROGRAMS; EXCLUDING OFFSETTING RECEIPTS)

Thus, the composition of federal spending has changed dramatically since 1965. Defense spending then accounted for 43.16 percent of federal spending, and Social Security accounted for 14.44 percent. Medicare accounted for 0 percent, Medicaid was 0.23 percent, other mandatory spending was 17.77 percent, and other discretionary spending was 2.64 percent.[27] In particular, health care spending was close to zero.[28] Starting in the mid-1960s, however, health care expenditure (consisting mainly of Medicare, Medicaid, disability and retirement spending, the Children's Health Insurance Program, and health insurance subsidies) began to grow, reaching 23.71 percent of expenditure in 2014.[29] At the same time, Social Security grew significantly, reaching about 24 percent of total federal spending and 5 percent of GDP in 2014. Thus, health care plus retirement spending is now 63.4 percent of total spending, while national defense is only 15.99 percent, and total discretionary is only 30.44 percent.[30,31]

An additional change in the nature of federal spending, concomitant with the first, has been the shift from discretionary to mandatory programs. Congress sets discretionary spending each year in annual appropriations bills. Discretionary spending consists mainly of defense, which was 48.6 percent of total discretionary in 2014. Other major components include transportation (7.6 percent), education (6.1 percent), veterans' benefits (5.4 percent), and international affairs (4.2 percent).[32]

Mandatory spending is set by laws that allow such spending to continue indefinitely unless Congress modifies the law. Mandatory spending consists mainly of Social Security (40.3 percent of total mandatory spending in 2014), Medicare (24.1 percent), Medicaid (14.4 percent), federal employee retirement and disability (6.4 percent), Supplemental Nutrition Assistance Program (4.6 percent), veterans' benefits (4.1 percent), earned income tax credit (2.9 percent), Supplemental Security Income

---

[27] Ibid.

[28] Other mandatory spending included some health expenditure in 1965.

[29] Congressional Budget Office, *2015 Long-Term Budget Outlook*.

[30] Ibid.

[31] Total federal spending consists of the following components: discretionary spending (defense spending and nondefense spending) and mandatory spending (Social Security, Medicare, Medicaid, income security, other retirement and disability programs, and other programs).

[32] Congressional Budget Office, *2015 Long-Term Budget Outlook*.

(2.4 percent), unemployment insurance (2.0 percent), and health insurance subsidies (0.4 percent). See Appendix B, Table 2, for further details.[33]

Given those changes in the composition of federal spending, the case can plausibly be made that spending will continue to grow faster than GDP in the future. The shift from national defense and other discretionary spending to health care and retirement spending represents a change from controversial spending to "popular" spending. The shift to mandatory spending means that a greater portion of federal expenditure can increase from year to year without new legislation or agreement between Democrats and Republicans. Such increases are likely because the aging of America's population means that a higher and higher proportion of the population is eligible for these mandatory programs. Plus, health care subsidies tend to raise health care prices, which further increases spending.

Figures 13 and 14 present the Congressional Budget Office's projections of discretionary and mandatory spending, respectively, over the next 75 years. Consistent with the reasoning above, those figures show stable discretionary spending but persistently increasing mandatory spending, especially for Medicare and Medicaid. Whether the projections will prove accurate depends on economic and demographic variables such as real GDP growth, wage rates, health care cost inflation, birth and death rates, immigration rates, and more. Deviations from the projections can be too pessimistic or too optimistic.

A possible caveat about such projections is that since the early 2000s, health care cost inflation has moderated substantially in the United States. The reasons for this slowdown are not fully understood, but they predate the recession and the Affordable Care Act, so those two factors are at a minimum not the whole story. If this slowdown continues over the long term, that change will moderate the growth in government health care expenditure and therefore imply smaller estimates of fiscal imbalance.[34]

For several reasons, however, this "good news" should be taken with a large grain of salt. Health care cost inflation slowed in the early 1990s but then accelerated again. Some of the growth of federal health care expenditure reflects demographics rather than health care cost inflation. As the baby boom generation retires and life expectancy increases,

---

[33] Congressional Research Service, *Mandatory Spending Since 1962*, CRS-7-5700 (Washington, D.C., 2015), https://www.fas.org/sgp/crs/misc/RL33074.pdf.

[34] See Chandra Amitabh, Jonathan Holmes, and Jonathan Skinner, "Is This Time Different? The Slowdown in Health Care Spending," *Brookings Paper on Economic Activity*, Fall 2013, pp. 261–311.

the fraction of the population receiving Medicare will continue to grow, implying rising expenditure even with less health care cost inflation. Moreover, the most recent data on health insurance premiums suggest substantially faster health care cost inflation over at least the next year

Figure 13
CBO Projections of Total Discretionary Spending as a Percentage of GDP

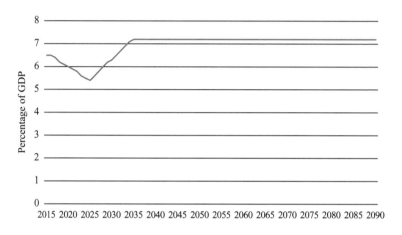

Figure 14
CBO Projections of Total Mandatory Spending as a Percentage of GDP

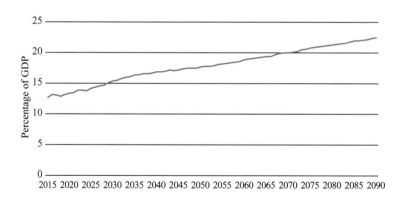

or so. In fact, Bureau of Labor Statistics data from early 2015 showed surprisingly large monthly jumps in the cost of hospital services.[35] And even projections that incorporate less rapid health care cost inflation still show Medicare and other health care expenditure growing faster than GDP by enough to make fiscal imbalance large.[36,37]

The CBO's projections make clear why, as noted earlier, the debt-to-GDP ratio is an incomplete picture of fiscal health: the debt accounts for past spending and taxation but ignores future spending or future ability to raise revenue.[38] Similarly, the existing debt-to-GDP ratio takes no account of the economy's future growth. If expenditure growth slows sufficiently relative to current projections or if the economy grows faster than current projections, implying greater revenue, then the debt ratio could decline enough to avoid fiscal difficulties. A complete picture of fiscal health must therefore integrate both past and future, and it must combine all the components of fiscal health quantitatively.

An Estimation of Fiscal Imbalance over Time

To show the quantitative effect of changes in U.S. fiscal policy over time, I estimate fiscal imbalance for each year starting in 1965. I start

---

[35] Dan Mangan, "Medical Cost Inflation: Highest Level in 8+ Years," CNBC.com, May 22, 2015, http://www.cnbc.com/2015/05/22/medical-cost-inflation-highest-level-in-8-years.html.

[36] See Douglas Elmendorf, "Comment," *Brookings Paper on Economic Activity,* Fall 2013, pp. 311–19.

[37] The CBO's baseline debt projections assume a 1.4 percent annual rate of health care excess cost growth, a rate that declines gradually to zero for Medicaid and to 1.0 percent for Medicare over the next 75 years. Those rates would be much lower than average health care cost inflation over the past two decades. Even given the conservative assumptions, however, the CBO still forecasts that 8 percent of GDP will be spent on major health care programs by 2040. For more information, see Congressional Budget Office, "Summary," *Long-Term Budget Outlook.*

[38] See Laurence J. Kotlikoff, "Deficit Delusion," *Public Interest* 84 (1986): 53–65; Laurence J. Kotlikoff, *Generational Accounting: Knowing Who Pays, and When, for What We Spend* (New York: Free Press, 1992); Laurence J. Kotlikoff, "From Deficit Delusion to the Fiscal Balance Rule: Looking for an Economically Meaningful Way to Assess Fiscal Policy," *The Journal of Economics* 58, no. 1 (1993): 17–41; and Alan J. Auerbach and Laurence J. Kotlikoff, *Dynamic Fiscal Policy* (Cambridge, England: Cambridge University Press, 1987). An important theme in this literature is that fiscal imbalances typically imply large redistributions across generations, with future generations facing substantially higher taxes to pay for the retirement and health care benefits of existing retirees. I abstract from those issues here. For an excellent discussion, see Alan J. Auerbach, Jagadeesh Gokhale, and Laurence J. Kotlikoff, "Generational Accounting: A Meaningful Way to Evaluate Fiscal Policy," *Journal of Economic Perspectives* (1994): 73–94.

1965

then because the data considered earlier suggest the United States had no serious issue of fiscal imbalance before that date. Further, the data necessary to construct the fiscal imbalance estimates are more readily available starting in 1965.

Fiscal imbalance (FI) is a measure of government financial health that, at a point in time, accounts for both explicit debt (the sum of all past deficits and surpluses, plus interest payments on the debt) and implicit debt (the expected value of all future deficits and surpluses, adjusted for the time value of money using present value).[39] Formally,

Fiscal Imbalance = Present Value of Future Expenditure –
Present Value of Future Revenue + Outstanding Debt

Calculation of fiscal imbalance requires projections of future spending and revenue, starting from each date for which one calculates FI, plus an assumed interest rate with which to discount future inflows and outflows.[40] I construct projections based on simplifying assumptions that allow clean analysis of the issues underlying the estimates.

As a first step, I create projections for real GDP, starting in 1965 and going forward as far as necessary. Those projections are calculated by taking actual real GDP in 1965, followed by 2.55 percent growth every year thereafter.[41] This assumed growth rate matches the average of the actual growth rate of real GDP over the past 40 years and the CBO's own long-term projections for GDP growth over the next 75 years.[42] (For consistency, throughout this model I use actual growth rates over the past four decades as well as CBO projections for the next 75 years to project future revenue and spending trajectories). This approach does *not* "reset" every year; that is, it does not assume 2.55 percent growth starting from the actual value of real GDP in each start year. Instead,

---

[39] For details, see "Fiscal Imbalance: A Primer," the first essay in this volume. Also refer to Kotlikoff, "Deficit Delusion"; Kotlikoff, *Generational Accounting*; Kotlikoff, "From Deficit Delusion to the Fiscal Balance Rule"; and Auerbach and Kotlikoff, *Dynamic Fiscal Policy.*

[40] Ideally, one calculates the present values over the infinite future. Under the assumptions used here, however, the present values over the infinite future are unbounded. I therefore use a 75-year horizon.

[41] The CBO's long-term budget forecast for 2015 projects a real growth rate of 2.3 percent for the next 75 years. Over the past 40 years, however, GDP growth has been 2.8 percent per year. The average of those two figures is 2.55 percent, the assumed growth rate here.

[42] Bureau of Economic Analysis, *National Income and Product Account Tables* (Washington, D.C.: U.S. Department of Commerce, 2015), http://www.bea.gov/iTable/index_nipa.cfm.

this approach creates one series for projected GDP, starting in 1965, and then uses that series for all future projections. The reason is to abstract out booms and recessions and instead to focus attention on how changes in spending or tax policies have changed fiscal imbalance.

Given those projected values for real GDP, I construct projections for revenue and discretionary spending by assuming they always equal 17.3 percent and 8.2 percent of real GDP, respectively. The values equal the average revenue-over-GDP and discretionary-spending-over-GDP ratios, respectively, between 1975 and 2014.[43]

The growth model for mandatory spending is constructed differently. The projections for Social Security for each start year equal actual spending on Social Security in that year, followed by 2.58 percent real growth per year for the next 75 years.[44] The average annual growth rate in real Social Security expenditure for the 1965–2014 period was 2.49 percent.[45] This figure is close to CBO projections, which predict that Social Security spending will increase at an average pace of 2.6 percent per year over the next 75 years.

The projections for Medicare and Medicaid are calculated using the same method as for Social Security, but with different spending growth rates. Medicare and Medicaid spending for each start year equals the actual value in that year followed by 4.58 percent and 4.29 percent real growth per year, respectively. The assumptions are derived by averaging the growth of Medicare and Medicaid spending over the past several decades with CBO projections for future decades.[46] Here, too, the approach is different than for real GDP, because the projection of future

[43] Congressional Budget Office, "January 2015 Baseline," *Budget and Economic Outlook: 2015 to 2025*, CBO-49892 (Washington, D.C., 2015), https://www.cbo.gov/publication/45249.

[44] I can illustrate this point with an example: if we were to project Social Security spending from the year 1990 onward, we would take the actual real expenditure in 1990 ($446.5 billion), then multiply that by 1.03 (i.e., a 3 percent annual growth rate) to get an estimate for spending in 1991 ($459.9 billion), in 1992 ($473.7 billion), and so on each year for the next 75 years. Together, those projections are used to calculate an estimate of fiscal imbalance in the year 1990. To calculate an estimate of fiscal imbalance in 1991, we would repeat the pattern using real Social Security spending from that "start year."

[45] Congressional Budget Office, "January 2015 Baseline."

[46] Those growth rates differ slightly from those offered by the CBO and other literature (e.g., Jagadeesh Gokhale, "Spending Beyond Our Means: How We Are Bankrupting Future Generations," Cato Institute White Paper, February 13, 2013), http://object.cato.org/sites/cato.org/files/pubs/pdf/spending-beyond-our-means.pdf. The CBO assumes a 4 percent growth rate for Medicare and a 3 percent growth rate for Medicaid over the

growth starts fresh from each projection date's actual value. This approach allows the present values to reflect the fact that those programs have expanded in scope over time.

I further include projections for mandatory spending on other programs. Lumped into this category are components such as unemployment insurance, the Supplemental Nutrition Assistance Program (formerly known as food stamps), retirement and disability programs, benefit programs for veterans, Medicare-Eligible Retiree Health Care Fund, ACA subsidies, federal student loan subsidies, and the Children's Health Insurance Program. Combined, those other programs account for roughly 30–35 percent of mandatory spending each year. Projections are calculated in a fashion parallel to Social Security, Medicare, and Medicaid. Spending for each start year equals the actual value in that year followed by 2.37 percent growth per year.

Next, to estimate fiscal imbalance, I calculate for each projection start year the present value of projected revenue and of each major expenditure component over the subsequent 75 years.[47] I then sum the present values of the expenditure projections, subtract the present value of the revenue projection, and add the explicit debt. This number gives an estimate of fiscal imbalance as of that start year. All present values assume a real interest rate of 3.22 percent, which equals the average real interest rate on 30-year long-term government bonds in the United States over the past four decades.[48]

Figure 15 plots the results. As of 1965, the assumptions made here imply a fiscal *balance* of $6.92 trillion expressed in terms of 2014 dollars. In other words, projected discounted revenue exceeded projected discounted spending by that amount. Thus the U.S. fiscal plan was sustainable at that time. Starting around that time, however, fiscal balance began a gradual but persistent deterioration, and balance had become imbalance by 1969. Around 2000, fiscal imbalance started to deepen more swiftly, caused in part by an acceleration in Medicare expenditures. In the wake of the Great Recession in 2008–2009, fiscal imbalance

---

next 75 years. This discrepancy may be one reason that my estimates for fiscal imbalance are larger than previous estimates.

[47] As noted, I use a 75-year rather than an infinite horizon because the latter is unbounded.

[48] The average real rate on long-term (30-year) government bonds was 3.2 percent over the past 40 years. See Federal Reserve Bank of St. Louis, Economic Data (2015), http://www.research.stlouisfed.org.

worsened because of a spike in Medicaid expenditures and other health care program costs. As of 2014, my assumptions produce an estimated imbalance of $117.9 trillion.[49]

The main improvement in FI occurs in 2010. Indeed, for 2010, the fiscal situation ameliorated from an imbalance of $129.59 trillion to $118.42 trillion. This improvement is a break with the previous 20-year downward trend, which plausibly reflects a reversal of exceptionally large federal spending during the Great Recession, particularly for income security programs and Medicaid. The slowdown in the growth of health care costs may have also played a role, though the CBO believes health care costs will pick back up according to recent data. In any case, the fiscal gains made in 2010 have not continued.

Overall, the main drivers of America's fiscal deterioration appear to be the ever-growing costs associated with Medicare, Medicaid, and other health programs. Whereas Social Security has accounted for a relatively constant share of expenditure in proportion to GDP, Medicare and Medicaid costs have been growing as a ratio of GDP for the past four decades. This growth is what makes the country's fiscal path unsustainable.

The estimates in Figure 15 rely on assumptions about future growth, revenue, spending, and interest rates. Sufficiently large changes in those assumptions can generate far less gloomy projections. Figures 16–20 show, however, that modifications over the plausible range do not change the main story. Figure 16 considers a real GDP growth rate 0.5 percent higher or lower, Figure 17 considers a real interest rate 0.5 percent higher or lower, Figure 18 considers growth rates for Medicare and Medicaid 1 percent higher or lower, Figure 19 considers raising or lowering discretionary spending as a share of GDP by 1 percent, and Figure 20 considers raising or lowering tax revenues as a share of GDP by 1 percent. None of those variations on the assumptions change the basic message: U.S. fiscal imbalance has been growing for several decades and is now larger than it has ever historically been.

---

[49] For comparison, other literature estimates the imbalance at $79.4 billion as of 2010. See Jagadeesh Gokhale and Kent Smetters, "Fiscal and Generational Imbalances: An Update," *Tax Policy and the Economy* 20 (2006): 193–223, http://www.nber.org/chapters/c0066.pdf. A more recent study by Gokhale estimates fiscal imbalance in 2014 at $94.9 trillion under CBO's alternative policies. For more, see Gohkale, "Spending Beyond Our Means," p. 12.

Figure 15
Projected Fiscal Imbalance (baseline assumptions)

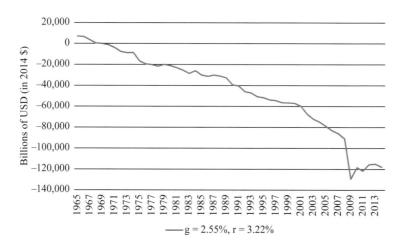

Figure 16
Fiscal Imbalance with Varying GDP Growth Rates

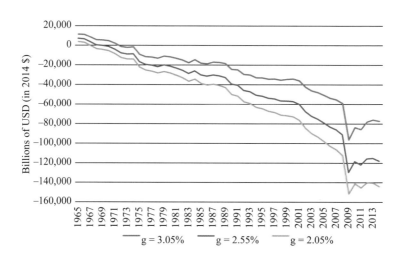

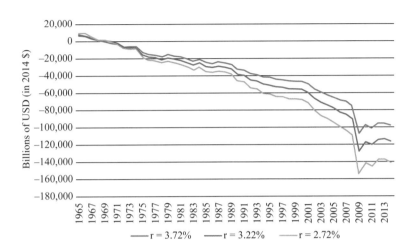

Figure 17
FISCAL IMBALANCE WITH VARYING INTEREST RATES

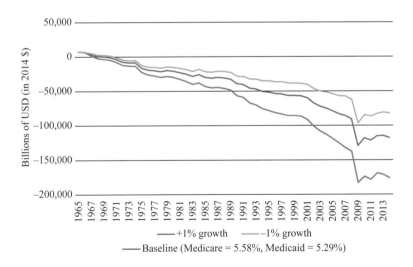

Figure 18
FISCAL IMBALANCE WITH VARYING MEDICARE AND MEDICAID
GROWTH RATES

Figure 19
FISCAL IMBALANCE WITH VARYING DISCRETIONARY SPENDING-TO-GDP
RATIOS

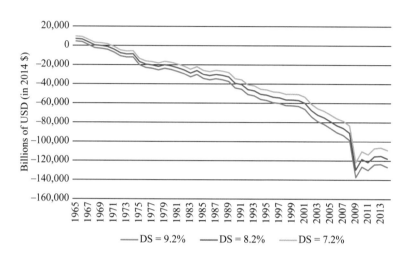

Figure 20
FISCAL IMBALANCE WITH VARYING REVENUE-TO-GDP RATIOS

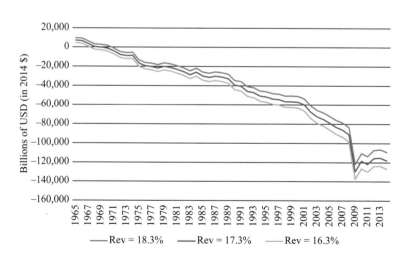

Discussion

The analysis presented here shows that until the 1930s, the United States faced no serious fiscal imbalance, it had not accumulated substantial explicit debt, and it had not adopted policies like Social Security or Medicare that generate implicit future liabilities. Prospects for continued economic growth, moreover, seemed good.

The situation changed somewhat in the 1930s and early 1940s. Certain policies adopted during the Great Depression—and especially WWII—generated greater spending, and the Great Depression reduced revenue. By the second half of the 1940s, the Great Depression and WWII turned out, however, to have been "transitory" shocks that did not by themselves cause permanent deterioration in fiscal health. Some policies adopted during the Depression implied higher expenditure on average (e.g., unemployment insurance) but not an ever-increasing expenditure relative to GDP.

Over the first two decades after WWII, fiscal health generally improved. Social Security expenditure increased relative to GDP, but the decline in defense expenditure combined with solid GDP growth implied that deficits were small on average, so the debt ratio declined.

Starting in 1965, however, Medicare, Medicaid, and more recently the ACA added the potential for major expansions of expenditure relative to output, and subsequent experience has confirmed this potential. By 2014, America's present-value fiscal imbalance, calculated over a 75-year horizon, had reached 797 percent of GDP.

In principle, the United States has three options for restoring fiscal balance: adopting policies that promote faster growth, raising taxes, or slowing the growth in expenditure.

In practice, as the estimates just described indicate, only expenditure cuts can make a significant difference. Faster growth is always desirable, other things being equal, though many current policies are both ill-advised and inimical to growth. Yet as Figure 16 shows, even a substantial increase in the growth rate would make only a moderate difference to fiscal imbalance, and adjusting policy sufficiently to achieve this growth rate would likely prove politically difficult. Similarly, Figure 20 suggests that even with tax revenue substantially above its postwar average, and assuming no effect on growth, fiscal imbalance would still be large. If higher taxes have even a modest negative impact on growth, tax increases have no capacity for restoring fiscal balance.

That finding leaves expenditure cuts—especially to Medicare, Medicaid, and ACA subsidies—as the only viable avenues for significant reductions in fiscal imbalance. Figure 21 shows the estimates of fiscal imbalance if all mandatory spending grew at a rate of just 2.55 percent—that is, the same rate as GDP. Under those assumptions, fiscal imbalance becomes substantially smaller.[50] Such large cuts are politically difficult given that the programs benefit a huge fraction of Americans, but they would indeed diminish fiscal imbalance. The crucial difference between cuts in expenditure and tax hikes is that the former could plausibly increase economic growth, or at worst have a minor effect, while the latter almost certainly reduce growth, making imbalance worse.[51]

Figure 21

FISCAL IMBALANCE WITH STABLE MANDATORY SPENDING GROWTH
(2.55 PERCENT)

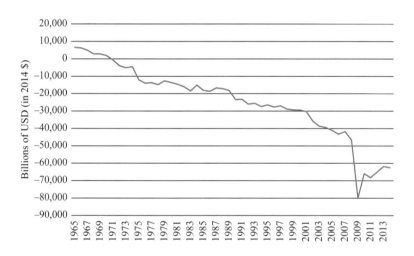

[50] The magnitude of fiscal imbalance shrinks by about half in those circumstances. Even though mandatory spending equals GDP growth in this scenario, fiscal imbalance does not fall to zero because current expenditure still outpaces revenue, so a "stable growth" scenario merely maintains the status quo. If one were to actually erase the fiscal imbalance, mandatory spending programs would have to grow at a rate slower than GDP growth.

[51] For overviews on how tax cuts and hikes can affect economic growth, see Christina Romer, "The Case for Fiscal Stimulus: The Likely Effects of the American Recovery and Reinvestment Act," Chair's Remarks, U.S. Monetary Policy Forum, New York, February 27, 2009. See also Mark Zandi, chief economist and cofounder of Moody's Economy.com,

Thus, cutting the growth of federal health expenditure is a win-win for the economy because it reduces fiscal imbalance and enhances the efficiency of the health care system at the same time.

Testimony before the Joint Economic Committee, October 29, 2009, "The Impact of the Recovery Act on Economic Growth," https://www.economy.com/mark-zandi/documents/JEC-Fiscal-Stimulus-102909.pdf.

Appendix A: Total Discretionary Spending, Defense Spending, and Other Discretionary Spending

Table 1

DISCRETIONARY OUTLAYS, FISCAL YEARS 2014–2015

	Billions of Dollars		Percent of GDP		Percent of Total Expenditures	
	2014	2015	2014	2015	2014	2015
National defense						
Department of Defense/military	572.71	560.83	3.32	3.14	16.33	15.25
Other defense	23.74	27.79	0.14	0.16	0.68	0.76
Subtotal	**596.45**	**588.62**	**3.46**	**3.30**	**17.01**	**16.01**
Nondefense						
International affairs	49.60	55.16	0.29	0.31	1.41	1.50
General science, space, and technology	28.47	29.75	0.16	0.17	0.81	0.81
Energy	5.43	7.34	0.03	0.04	0.15	0.20
Natural resources and environment	35.60	38.11	0.21	0.21	1.02	1.04
Agriculture	5.54	7.03	0.03	0.04	0.16	0.19
Commerce and housing credit	−6.83	−4.89	−0.04	−0.03	−0.19	−0.13
Transportation	89.99	33.49	0.52	0.19	2.57	0.91
Community and regional development	22.04	25.47	0.13	0.14	0.63	0.69
Education, employment, and social services	92.10	93.22	0.53	0.52	2.63	2.54
Health	55.73	59.82	0.32	0.34	1.59	1.63
Medicare	6.39	6.43	0.04	0.04	0.18	0.17
Income security	64.21	67.34	0.37	0.38	1.83	1.83
Social Security	5.66	5.54	0.03	0.03	0.16	0.15
Veterans' benefits and services	63.13	64.69	0.37	0.36	1.80	1.76
Administration of justice	49.41	51.94	0.29	0.29	1.41	1.41

Continued on p. 66

General government	15.76	17.08	0.09	0.10	0.45	0.46
Subtotal	**582.22**	**557.52**	**3.37**	**3.12**	**16.61**	**15.16**
Total discretionary outlays	**1,178.67**	**1,146.14**	**6.83**	**6.42**	**33.62**	**31.17**

Source: Office of Management and Budget, *Historical Tables, Table 8.7: Outlays for Discretionary Programs* (Washington, D.C., 2015), https://www.whitehouse.gov/sites/default/files/omb/budget/fy2016/assets/hist08z7.xls.

Appendix B: Total Mandatory Spending, Social Security, Medicare, Medicaid, and Other Mandatory Spending Programs

Table 2
MANDATORY OUTLAYS, FISCAL YEARS 2014–2015

	Billions of Dollars		Percent of GDP		Percent of Total Expenditures	
	2014	2015	2014	2015	2014	2015
Social Security						
Old-Age and Survivors Insurance	702.91	738.29	4.07	4.14	20.05	20.08
Disability Insurance	141.97	143.72	0.82	0.81	4.05	3.91
Subtotal	**844.88**	**882.01**	**4.89**	**4.94**	**24.10**	**23.99**
Major health care programs						
Medicare	599.81	639.02	3.47	3.58	17.11	17.38
Medicaid	301.47	350.12	1.75	1.96	8.60	9.52
Health insurance subsidies and related spending	14.87	36.94	0.09	0.21	0.42	1.00
Children's Health Insurance Program	9.31	9.04	0.05	0.05	0.27	0.25
Subtotal	**925.47**	**1,035.12**	**5.36**	**5.80**	**26.40**	**28.15**
Income security						
Earned income, child, and other tax credits	86.01	84.94	0.50	0.48	2.45	2.31
Supplemental Nutrition Assistance Program	76.24	76.32	0.44	0.43	2.17	2.08
Supplemental Security Income	54.04	54.85	0.31	0.31	1.54	1.49
Unemployment compensation	43.89	33.49	0.25	0.19	1.25	0.91
Family support and foster care	30.75	30.85	0.18	0.17	0.88	0.84
Child nutrition	20.00	21.66	0.12	0.12	0.57	0.59
Subtotal	**310.93**	**302.12**	**1.80**	**1.69**	**8.87**	**8.22**

Continued on p. 68

Federal civilian and military retirement						
Civilian	93.68	96.62	0.54	0.54	2.67	2.63
Military	55.35	56.62	0.32	0.32	1.58	1.54
Other	8.47	6.65	0.05	0.04	0.24	0.18
Subtotal	**157.51**	**159.89**	**0.91**	**0.90**	**4.49**	**4.35**
Veterans						
Income security	70.94	75.85	0.41	0.43	2.02	2.06
Other	15.82	16.07	0.09	0.09	0.45	0.44
Subtotal	**86.76**	**91.92**	**0.50**	**0.52**	**2.47**	**2.50**
Other programs						
Agriculture	19.19	13.28	0.11	0.07	0.55	0.36
Medicare-Eligible Retiree Health Care Fund	9.26	10.03	0.05	0.06	0.26	0.27
Deposit insurance	−13.85	−10.23	−0.08	−0.06	−0.40	−0.28
Fannie Mae and Freddie Mac	0	0				
Higher education	−11.97	21.35	−0.07	0.12	−0.34	0.58
Other	51.73	59.67	0.30	0.33	1.48	1.62
Subtotal	**54.35**	**94.10**	**0.31**	**0.53**	**1.55**	**2.56**
Offsetting receipts						
Medicare	−94.51	−98.47	−0.55	−0.55	−2.70	−2.68
Federal share of federal employees' retirement	−65.36	−67.61	−0.38	−0.38	−1.86	−1.84
Fannie Mae and Freddie Mac	−74.39	−22.80	−0.43	−0.13	−2.12	−0.62
Other	−47.14	−79.07	−0.27	−0.44	−1.34	−2.15
Subtotal	**−281.39**	**−267.94**	**−1.63**	**−1.50**	**−8.03**	**−7.29**
Total mandatory outlays	**2,098.50**	**2,297.21**	**12.16**	**12.87**	**59.85**	**62.47**

Source: Congressional Budget Office, *The 2015 Long-Term Budget Outlook: January 2015 Baseline* (Washington, D.C., 2015), Table 3.2, https://www.cbo.gov/publication/45069.

About the Author

Jeffrey Miron is director of economic studies at the Cato Institute and director of undergraduate studies in the Department of Economics at Harvard University. His area of expertise is the economics of libertarianism, with particular emphasis on the economics of illegal drugs.

Miron has served on the faculty at the University of Michigan and as a visiting professor at the Sloan School of Management, MIT. From 1992 to 1998, he was chairman of the department of economics at Boston University. He is the author of *Drug War Crimes: The Consequences of Prohibition* and *The Economics of Seasonal Cycles*, in addition to numerous op-eds and journal articles. He has been the recipient of an Olin Fellowship from the National Bureau of Economic Research, an Earhart Foundation Fellowship, and a Sloan Foundation Faculty Research Fellowship.

Miron received a BA from Swarthmore College in 1979 and a PhD in economics from MIT in 1984.

Cato Institute

Founded in 1977, the Cato Institute is a public policy research foundation dedicated to broadening the parameters of policy debate to allow consideration of more options that are consistent with the principles of limited government, individual liberty, and peace. To that end, the Institute strives to achieve greater involvement of the intelligent, concerned lay public in questions of policy and the proper role of government.

The Institute is named for Cato's Letters, libertarian pamphlets that were widely read in the American Colonies in the early 18th century and played a major role in laying the philosophical foundation for the American Revolution.

Despite the achievement of the nation's Founders, today virtually no aspect of life is free from government encroachment. A pervasive intolerance for individual rights is shown by government's arbitrary intrusions into private economic transactions and its disregard for civil liberties. And while freedom around the globe has notably increased in the past several decades, many countries have moved in the opposite direction, and most governments still do not respect or safeguard the wide range of civil and economic liberties.

To address those issues, the Cato Institute undertakes an extensive publications program on the complete spectrum of policy issues. Books, monographs, and shorter studies are commissioned to examine the federal budget, Social Security, regulation, military spending, international trade, and myriad other issues. Major policy conferences are held throughout the year, from which papers are published thrice yearly in the *Cato Journal*. The Institute also publishes the quarterly magazine *Regulation*.

In order to maintain its independence, the Cato Institute accepts no government funding. Contributions are received from foundations, corporations, and individuals, and other revenue is generated from the sale of publications. The Institute is a nonprofit, tax-exempt, educational foundation under Section 501(c)3 of the Internal Revenue Code.

CATO INSTITUTE
1000 Massachusetts Ave., N.W.
Washington, D.C. 20001
www.cato.org